How to Get the Most Out of Coaching

A Client's Guide for Optimizing the Coaching Experience

By Karen Davis and Alex Mill

Praise for *How to Get the Most Out of Coaching, A Client's Guide for Optimizing the Coaching Experience*

Alex and Karen have turned coaching on its head, focusing on the leader's participation as an essential component of this process. As a coach for over 40 years, I recognized this book as a game-changer from the first page! Start getting the most out of your coaching, mentoring, and learning—a must read!

—Marshall Goldsmith, New York Times #1 Bestselling Author of *Triggers, Mojo,* **and** *What Got You Here Won't Get You There,* **Thinkers50 #1 Executive Coach, and the only two-time #1 Leadership Thinker in the world.**

If you've already been smart enough to hire a coach, I hope you're smart enough to read this book. If you don't, you risk wasting a powerful opportunity.

—Michael Bungay Stanier, Bestselling Author of *The Coaching Habit*

We are now in the Coaching Century and if you want to perform at the highest of levels—as an executive, an entrepreneur, or an athlete—you need world-class coaching. But that's actually only going to take you halfway… You see, coaching is a 200% relationship. A great coach trains for years to bring true magic to their coaching. But—until now—no one has shown a client how to bring their 100% to the table. If you are—or you want to be—a top performer, you need to filter for a world-class coach. And if you want your coaching to be extraordinary, you need to become a world-class client. Karen Davis and Alex Mill have written the guide you need. Read it now.

—Rich Litvin, Founder of Transition Excellence

What makes coaching a transformative life experience versus an exercise in going through the motions? YOU!! *How to Get the Most Out of Coaching* is your practical go-to guide for strengthening your coachability so you can be prepared, present, and ready to create within every coaching session. A must-read for anyone investing in coaching and ALL coaches!

—Melissa Ford, Coach, Author of *Living Service: The Journey of a Prosperous Coach*

Coaching has the power to create a positive impact on the world. I have seen that firsthand. In all the resources produced about coaching, there has been a tremendous focus on coaches themselves. Countless books, courses, and training to ensure they become the best. *How to Get the Most Out of Coaching* is unique. It turns the attention to the other side of the equation. This book teaches clients how to meet their coaches in a way that maximizes their results.

—Benjamin Croft, Chairman of The WBECS Group of companies (World Business & Executive Coach Summit), Philanthropist, Investor, INC 5000 and Dr. Marshall Goldsmith Award Recipient

The stigma of coaching has long passed as a liability. Now the world has accepted that high-performers and winners hire coaches to get even better. The downside is that the coaching field has proliferated like weeds, creating a massive quality range. Having decided to level up your game, don't waste your money on a bad experience. Davis and Mill have created a gift for you and all future coachees to make sure your investment in yourself is worthwhile, and that you select the coach that is best suited to you. Before you hire anyone, read this book.

—Ron Carucci, Managing Partner, Navalent, Author of *Rising to Power* and *To Be Honest*

What a gift to the world! If you want to get the most out of your coach, buy and read this book. If you are a coach, buy and read this book and gift it to all of your clients. If you are a leader, athlete, actor, doctor, or any professional who wants to improve your performance. Buy and read this book. The return on investment of this book cannot be overstated. This book is brilliant!

—Ankush Jain, Author of *Sweet Sharing, Rediscovering the Real You*

How to Get the Most Out of Coaching, A Client's Guide for Optimizing the Coaching Experience takes the reader on a never-before-seen tour of what it takes to be a powerful coaching client. While most books in the coaching profession look at the intricacies of being a good coach, Karen and Alex flip the coaching world on its head by sharing their valuable, engaging, and practical experience of how to be a world-class coaching client. The teachings in this book are transferable to every other aspect of life—including your relationships and business. And here's what I've learned over the years in the profession: You can't give what you don't have. The best coaches in the world have coaches themselves and are coachable. So if you're a coach and want to learn what it takes to be at the top of your game, this book is for you. You will learn what it takes to show up prepared, open, and curious in ways that can transform your life. In turn, you will have all it takes to show up and serve your own clients at your highest level of service.

—Devon Bandison, The Go-To Mind Coach of the NBA

Life-changing coaching doesn't just happen, even with a great coach. It also depends on what you bring to the party. Davis and Mill have drawn on their vast experience to create a gem of a book that shines with cogent stories, valuable principles, and doable steps for getting the most out of your coaching experience.

—Amy Hardison, Co-author of *The Ultimate Coach*

Hallelujah! For those of us who work with a coach, we have desperately needed a book like this. Over and over, Karen Davis and Alex Mill remind us that it's what WE, as clients, bring to our coaching conversations that helps create the changes we are looking for. This book does a brilliant job at giving us tools so we can get more from our coaching, show up to each conversation prepared and primed for the transformation we are hoping to experience… and they bring joy and fun into the teaching. This is a must read for every coach and anyone working with a coach.

—Tina Quinn, Life & Leadership Coach, Speaker, Author of *Invisible Things - The most important things in life are the ones you can't see*

Coaching is a resource-intensive undertaking. Karen Davis and Alex Mill are pros who have created an invaluable asset that will ensure you get the most out of your investment. This book addresses almost every scenario, from preparation to possible derailment. As a client, read this book first. As a coach, use this book to guide your clients to greater success.

—Mark J. Silverman, Author of *Only 10s 2.0 - Confront Your To-Do List and Transform Your Life*

Getting a career coach is an important step in the "business of you," but you can't stop there. Get smart, get prepared, and read this expert guidance from coaches Karen and Alex. You'll compound the value of your coaching, which will be the second-smartest step you'll take.

—**Jennifer Fondrevay, Founder, Day1 Ready M&A Consultancy, Best-selling Author of** *NOW WHAT? A Survivor's Guide for Thriving Through Mergers & Acquisitions*

How to Get the Most Out of Coaching is an extraordinary step-by-step guide on how to utilize coaching to receive the greatest transformation in any or all areas of your life. The examples and stories Karen and Alex provide throughout the book are so helpful for integration and implementation of all the wisdom they share. I only wish I'd had this book when I first started receiving coaching and being a coach! Highly recommend it for new and experienced coaches and their clients!

—**Kamin Samuel, Rapid Transformation Business & Executive Life Coach**

So many books are written about how to be a coach and how to improve coaching skills. Karen and Alex take a completely different approach and dive deep into what it takes to be an ultimate coaching client. They weave years of their personal experiences as coaches and coaching clients to offer tangible and actionable examples to support coaches and their clients. This book is as much for coaching clients as it is for coaches.

—**Yanush Cherkis, Executive Coach**

This is a must have for coaches to read for themselves (as most of us are also clients of coaching!) and to give to their clients! Whether you're a veteran of coaching, or new to it, this book is incredibly helpful to get the most out of the coaching experience. I wish I had this book several years ago, but the beauty of it is that we ALL have this book now and can create even more impactful and positive life changes for our clients as they are now empowered with the practical information they need to engage fully. Karen and Alex, you hit a big gap out there with this book. THANK YOU!

—**Dr. Laurie Addison, Executive & Leadership Development Coach**

Life is about getting comfortable by doing what makes you uncomfortable. The moment you start getting comfortable with the status quo, CHANGE! Karen and Alex's book is a good reminder that sometimes we need someone who can see the bigger picture when we ourselves can't (or won't). It's time to say PUT ME IN, COACH, instead of watching from the bench. Get in the game!

—Jeffrey Hayzlett, Primetime TV & Podcast Host, Speaker, Author, and Part-Time Cowboy

This is the book that I wish I would have had when I first became a coaching client! New coaching clients want to prepare for their sessions, but they need a guide to show them the way. *How To Get the Most Out of Coaching* is that guide that helps them to become amazing clients and understand how to take advantage of the coaching sessions in the best way possible.

—Susan M. Barber, Author of *The Visibility Factor*

There are numerous books written for coaches on how to coach, but none have been written on how to best prepare a client for a successful coaching relationship. This insightful book calls out the spotted elephant in the room and names the top places where clients get derailed from the true power of coaching. I will be sending copies as part of my on-boarding process to all of my clients.

—Gretchen Hydo, Master Coach

Aside from being incredibly helpful, this book is fun and easy to read. It highlights challenges you may not even be aware of that are blocking your ability to get the most out of coaching, and lovingly and simply offers small shifts that have a big impact. For both coaches and clients, this book is a game changer in terms of helping people access the level of transformation they're investing for! I would recommend this book to anyone receiving coaching of any kind (including athletic coaching) and anyone who is a client themselves. In just one chapter, I discovered several ways that I could increase the power of my work with both my clients and my coach. They knocked it out of the park!

—Vanessa Broers, Master Coach and Author of *We Are One: How one woman reclaimed her identity through motherhood*

A must read for every person investing in coaching! Karen and Alex share deep wisdom on how to fully be present in your transformation and growth when you invest in a coach, so you get the results you desire! It has become part of the recommended reading list for my clients!
—**Kami Guildner, Kami Guildner Coaching**

Karen Davis is the coach's coach. She is one of the few professional coaches that I have seen create deep impact and lasting change. With this book, you now get to have a glimpse of how Karen does her magic with her clients. You won't want to put the book down.
—**Amir Karkouti, Author of** *Lessons From My Coach: Become an Extraordinary Coach, Attract Extraordinary Clients* **and** *What the F**k Are the Three Principles?: And 18 Other Questions Answered from So-Called Wisdom*

As Karen's apprentice, and one of her "guinea pig" clients while this book was being written, I can attest to how the distilled wisdom in this book—if practiced—is like a cheat code for getting a high return from investment in coaching. The ideas and systems Karen developed from real experience helped me leverage coaching to create a very quick and profound transformation across all of the key aspects of my life: relationships, confidence, creative expression, finance, and professional performance. As an executive coach, working with driven entrepreneurs and busy high performers, I can attest to how the systems in this book have also helped my clients to go further in creating important changes across their lives. This book is now required reading for my clients.
—**Justin Perkins, Executive Coach, New Edge Advisors**

A first of its kind! I am not aware of another book that so well lays out a pathway for a great coaching relationship, from the CLIENT'S perspective. This book was well written and I am looking forward to it benefitting my clients' coaching experience.
—**Rachel Miller, MD, Pocket Bridges**

I've been looking forward to reading Karen and Alex's book, after having been coached by both of them during 2020. As I read their years of firsthand experience summarized simply and succinctly, one insight after another arose for me. In the moment of those insights, I was immediately able to apply new action to my existing coaching practice. If you are a coach, read this book. If you want to be coached, read this book.

—**Matt Hogan, Matt Hogan Worldwide**

This book is a must read for all coaches and coaching clients! I plan to give it to all my clients at the onset to set the foundation for a powerful coaching relationship and experience.

—**Kendra Dahlstrom, Corporate Leadership Development Coach and Facilitator**

How to Get the Most Out of Coaching

A Client's Guide for Optimizing the Coaching Experience

By Karen Davis and Alex Mill

How to Get the Most Out of Coaching, A Client's Guide for Optimizing the Coaching Experience by Karen Davis and Alex Mill

To contact the authors:
www.karendaviscoaching.com
www.zenlife.coach

For more information about bulk purchase discounts or publisher permissions, please contact Karen Davis at karen@karendaviscoaching.com

Cover design by Brendan Hemp, *HeavyLifting*, and Claire Lacy, *Pithy Wordsmithery*
Interior layout by Sue Murray, *Pithy Wordsmithery*
Copyediting by Chris Peters, *Pithy Wordsmithery*, and Jeff Marlin, *Marlin Creative*
Proofreading by Nils Kuehn, *Pithy Wordsmithery*

First Edition

Names and identifying details of some individuals in this book have been changed to protect their privacy.

Paperback ISBN: 978-1-7342391-8-8
Ebook ISBN: 978-1-7342391-9-5

Library of Congress Control Number: 2021916674

To Steve Chandler, with love and gratitude

Table of Contents

Foreword: Super-Powerful Client Engagement

Most people seek out coaching to fix or improve something in their lives. It's a rapidly trending profession, and they have had friends and colleagues who swear by it. They hire a coach and come to their first session with goals and challenges, hoping for the best. Then they sit back and wait for the coach to perform the transformational magic they have heard so much about.

However, early sessions with their coach are often slow going. They don't really know how to make the process work for themselves, so they sit back and wait. Their approach seems to be right out of the rock opera *Tommy* by The Who: "See me, feel me, touch me, heal me."

But there's a problem with that approach: They're only getting about 50 percent of the benefit from the coaching process when they enter it that way. This book brings it up close to 100 percent.

As you'll realize when you dive into this insightful and extremely useful field guide, successful coaching is an interactive process. It's a partnership, not a solo performance. It works best and gets the best results when the client is a full participant.

Karen Davis and Alex Mill are two of the most creative, devoted, and impactful coaches I know. Both have been powerful speakers at my live ACS (Advanced Client Systems) coaching schools over the years, and both are guest teachers in my online Coaching Prosperity School. The three of us teamed up to lead the live Reinventing Yourself Weekends. And all of Alex's books on Zen Buddhism and meditation are wonderful. They are always worth listening to.

Their collaboration in writing this book takes their service to the world to a new level. They have created an absolutely thorough and comprehensive guide for anyone entering or even considering entering into a coaching process.

I've seen and read every book I can find on coaching itself, but never until now have I encountered a book such as this—a book on how the other half of the equation works, how to be a good client! And how, as the title aptly states, to get the most out of working with a coach. And even though this book was written for the benefit of clients, it is equally valuable to coaches, providing better ways to serve deeply, especially at the beginning of the relationship.

We often hear how long it sometimes takes for a client to "get up to speed" and learn to fully engage in coaching sessions. I know this was true in my case. I'd often show up for sessions unprepared and clueless about what I wanted to work on.

Many of my own clients were the same way. They would show up thinking, What do I do? Should I talk about my fears and other feelings? How do I make the investment I've made in coaching pay off for me? Can I cancel sessions? Do I need to have huge goals?

I would have loved to have had this book back then to give to every client at the beginning of each relationship.

I'm glad this book exists now. It has the potential to transform an entire profession. When you read it, you'll see what I mean.

Steve Chandler
Birmingham, Michigan
March 2021

Preface: What Now?

Imagine you've just committed to paying a coach to help with your personal growth and success. You've also agreed to spend hours of precious time over many months in a process that, at this point, you might not fully understand. You're excited, but also anxious, and maybe even a little skeptical.

What now? How do you make the most out of your investment?

If this situation sounds familiar, know that you are not alone! One-on-one coaching can be a rewarding, transformative experience—but it can be hard to know what to expect. After years of coaching, we've seen firsthand how this lack of understanding impacts people's approach to their relationship with their coach, their commitment to the process, and ultimately, the results they experience.

As coaches, we have a burning desire to help people not only achieve their dreams and goals, but go beyond that. We want people to be utterly amazed by their progress. This drive isn't unique to us as coaches; this is a desire all coaches share. We are in your corner cheering you on, and we want nothing more than for you to create everything you want in your life.

After more than a decade of coaching a wide range of individuals and dedicating thousands of hours to our practice, we thought it might be time to write a book to instruct people (such as you) on the methods and mindsets that will empower them to get the most out of their coaching investment. There are so many books to help coaches be great, but none to help clients understand their role in the coaching relationship.

We ran our idea by the coaches in our network, and they loved it! They told us how dedicated they are to helping their clients, and how much they wished their clients knew the strategies that support exponential success, as well as the pitfalls that can impede progress. The issues that prevent people from getting the most out of coaching are complex. There are a lot of nuances to unpack here—and getting into the details would take several coaching sessions in and of itself.

Coaching is a two-way street, and we want to show you how to leverage your abilities, maximize your potential, and reap all the benefits of your coaching sessions. That's what inspired us to write this book. We saw that a resource was desperately needed to help people understand how to maximize their coaching experience.

Who We Are

Neither one of us ever set out to be a coach. When we were younger, coaching wasn't a job we even considered as a possible career path. Back then, the industry was still in its infancy. Athletes had coaches, but few people sought coaching outside of sports.

Decades later, things have changed dramatically. Many came to realize that if you want to get better at something—whether it's leadership, communication, or a jump shot—it pays to be intentional about your progress, and to get insight from others who are knowledgeable about the tasks you've set before yourself and can provide a different perspective on how to achieve them. Just like you can't watch yourself shooting a basketball to see where your form is off, you can't watch yourself leading a team of people and see yourself as they see you.

We've both been coaching in one form or another for many years, and we can't imagine a career better suited for us. In addition to being coauthors on this book, we are partners in life. We met in a coaches' training program in 2014, and the rest is history! We love serving others and helping people improve their lives and businesses. It's the kind of work that lights us up day after day.

Karen Davis

After 25 years in managerial and executive leadership roles in the business-to-business technology and services space, Karen made the decision to change her life by working to transform the lives of others. Consequently, she has been coaching, consulting, and facilitating leadership workshops for individuals, small businesses, and Fortune 100 companies for well over a decade now—and she is a Professionally Certified Coach through the International Coaching Federation (ICF). Today, her practice is mostly one-on-one deep coaching with executives, entrepreneurs, and executive coaches. Along the way, she's learned from some of the very best in the coaching business, including Steve Chandler, Rich Litvin, Steve Hardison, Byron Katie, Werner Erhard, Julio Olalla, and George and Linda Pransky. She also coauthored two other books—*When All Boats Rise: 12 Coaches on Service as the Heart of a Thriving Practice* and *Unconventional Wisdom: Stories Beyond the Mind to Awaken the Heart*—that focus on leading and serving.

Alex Mill

Alex trained at a Zen Buddhist monastery for nearly 14 years, during which time he spent more than 10,000 hours in meditation. There, he learned how his own thoughts kept him stuck and how he could access freedom to authentically succeed in all areas of his life. When he ultimately left the monastery, he took many of the teachings with him and actually built them into his own coaching practice. Today, he focuses on helping people achieve success both powerfully and peacefully. The idea for this book was born out of Alex's understanding of how resistance and sabotage can prevent people from getting what they want, and how to overcome that.

Introduction:
Your Guide for How to Get
the Most Out of Coaching

One-on-one coaching can transform both your career and personal life. Whether you want to become more successful at work, deepen your relationships with the people who matter most, or break free from unproductive patterns, working with a coach can help you create the life you've always wanted. We call this the "created future" because it's a path you intentionally choose for yourself. Your created future can be in stark contrast to your "default future," which is the place your life is headed, whether you're obliviously on autopilot or constantly in reaction mode. In your created future, anything is possible.

Over the years, our clients have achieved astonishing results—and we are deeply passionate about the work we do because we see the impact it makes. We've helped clients become more-effective leaders, which has translated into hundreds of thousands of dollars in additional revenue in their businesses. We've worked with executives to help them ask for higher salaries and better compensation packages. Our clients have gained the clarity and awareness to save their marriages, get their health back on track, and rekindle meaningful relationships with estranged loved ones.

That said, coaching isn't a magic bullet. All too often, people have the desire to improve, but fail to make the exponential growth they so desperately deserve. It isn't always because their goals are unattainable or they aren't getting the right support from their coach; it's due to them not knowing how to get the most out of coaching. In other words, certain actions make a radical difference in results.

After reflecting on our many years of coaching, we've identified the processes and habits that make people successful, as well as the root causes of slow progress. Working with our wide range of clients, from successful entrepreneurs to Fortune 100 executives to individuals who were simply looking for more peace and balance in a hectic world, we've seen how some people surpass all their goals and expectations, while others take longer than necessary to realize meaningful progress.

That's where this book comes in. It is a straightforward guide to ensure you get the absolute biggest benefits from your one-on-one coaching relationship.

But before we dive in, it's important to make sure we're on the same page when it comes to the basics.

What Is Coaching?

Coaching is about moving forward and preparing for the future. Think of a professional golfer or tennis star. These athletes rely on coaches to bring out their best performance. Examine the results and you'll see that the best professional coaches train the whole athlete—combining physical, psychological, and spiritual aspects to support their clients' personal growth. A good coach nurtures your untapped potential, moving you to ever-higher levels of responsibility and accountability—at times beyond your comfort zone—to help you reach your goals.

In coaching, the fundamental belief is that you are capable of creating your own solutions—it's not up to your coach. By contrast, traditional counseling and psychotherapy typically focus on resolving issues rooted in the past, such as abuse, addiction, and trauma. Counseling strives to heal psychological and/or physical conditions, with the goal of reaching a healthier emotional state and achieving overall well-being.

Consultants are different from coaches, too. They offer specialized expertise and prescribed solutions in order to "fix" issues. Goals are often based on business objectives such as increasing revenue, improving productivity, or mastering the skills needed for a new role. In a consulting relationship, you pose a problem or deficiency and the consultant applies their expertise to recommend a solution and define action items. There may be some tailoring of best practices to the individual, but the goal of consulting is to lead you down a particular path rather than help you discover your own best path. Additionally, consultants are not expected to advise clients beyond the identified issue, whereas coaching tends to have an integrated, whole-person approach.

What Is a Coach's Role?

First and foremost, coaches honor you as the expert in your own life and work, understanding that every client is creative, resourceful, and whole. A coach's role is to give you the tools and resources you need to better navigate your personal and professional life. Trained to listen, observe, and customize an approach to fit your unique needs, your coach should encourage you to explore and understand the barriers that keep you from reaching your full potential.

Coaches come with a lot of different backgrounds and approaches. But a coach should always be your own personal champion, cheering you on and helping you reach your goals. Good coaches guide you through a thought-provoking self-discovery process, inspiring you to find the path that maximizes your personal and professional potential.

Types of Coaching

Your coach's background and experience can be excellent indicators of whether they are the right match for you. Many coaches focus on a specific niche, specializing in leadership, relationships, small business growth, creativity/innovation, or mindfulness. Some coach holistically, seeking to help you make improvements across all areas of your life. Other coaches specialize in working with certain demographics, such as teenagers, doctors, executives, entrepreneurs, women, or new mothers. Sometimes coaches set up their practice to intentionally focus on these areas or segments of the population, and other times it happens organically as they gain more experience working with specific types of clients. For example, Alex, having spent 14 years in a Zen Buddhist monastery training in mindfulness, is an expert in helping his clients move beyond their inner chatter and into powerful self-expressed freedom. This is a bit different from Karen, who specializes in working with executives and entrepreneurs on the landscape of life and career.

Unlike other industries that have been around for centuries, coaching is fairly new and unregulated. There are coaching certification programs through organizations such as ICF, and coaching schools can be highly beneficial for coaches, but the industry is currently more focused on learning through apprenticeships, much like with engineers, paramedics, and carpenters. In other words, coaches are most often taught directly by other coaches. Karen works with a handful of executive coaches in an apprenticeship relationship in which she focuses on advising, teaching, and coaching to enhance their own skills and improve their businesses.

Formats and Durations

Coaching programs come in all types, and there's a great deal of variation in the total length of contracts. A common format consists of biweekly sessions, during which you and your coach meet for one hour. Some coaches only take on new clients for specific durations in time, such as six months or a year. In addition to weekly sessions, other formats include one- or two-day deep dives, weekend retreats, weeklong retreats, and 15-minute daily power sessions. These might be conducted over the phone or via video conferencing, in person at your coach's studio, or at a special location. For example, Karen offers one-hour sessions the first three weeks of each month, in-person two-day Accelerators, and one-day equine-guided sessions wherein clients meet with her at a horse ranch for a day of groundwork and inner exploration.

So how do you know what's right for you? The best way to assess whether you and your potential coach are a good fit for one another is to ask them for an example of what it would be like for you to be in a coaching relationship with them based on their typical experiences with clients.

Accountability

After your sessions, you may walk away with specific action items. These may include tasks to complete, books to read, or simple practices such as working to change the way you communicate. Some coaches will hold you accountable for taking action. They might have you fill out a form on which you check off your action points and share what you did. Or they might begin sessions by asking you how you moved forward with your objectives from the previous week. Other coaches don't focus on accountability because they believe it's their client's responsibility. Neither approach is right or wrong, but it's good to talk with your coach about this up front so you know what to expect. (More on this in "Chapter 6: Setting Ground Rules.")

Investment

Coaching takes time, money, and emotional commitment. Just like there's a massive range in the types of coaching, format, and duration, the same is true when it comes to cost. Coaches with less experience may be very affordable, whereas those who have international demand charge substantial fees. Few things in life offer any kind of guaranteed return on investment, but the rewards of coaching often far outweigh the risks.

What You Can Expect to Learn in This Book:

How to Set the Right Goals

The most meaningful goals we could set for ourselves might not be the ones we gravitate toward initially. That's because our deepest desires aren't always hanging out on the surface. Using powerful reflection questions, we help you identify what will give you the greatest reward from coaching. From there, we show you how to work with your coach to create a road map to reach your goals.

What to Do Before, During, and After Your Coaching Sessions

To get the most out of coaching, you need to start by optimizing your time. We'll explain how to show up to your sessions prepared and to leverage that highly valuable time before and after speaking with your coach. Our simple best practices for time management have made a world of difference for our clients, and we're excited to share them with you.

The Difference Between Inner and Outer Work

There are different ways to think about personal transformation. Some people want to become more mindful and cultivate a greater sense of inner peace. Others seek to boost their income by $100K in one year. We find that these kinds of goals are typically more closely related than people realize. We will show how taking a hybrid approach to inner and outer transformation often yields the best results.

The Traits That Improve Your Coachability

After years of coaching others and being coached ourselves, we identified a list of key traits inextricably linked to better outcomes. Most people naturally exhibit at least a few of these traits in their sessions, and can easily cultivate others with a little mindfulness and intention. We'll teach you what to watch out for so you can keep an eye on your own tendencies and improve how you show up.

Applying What You've Learned

Gaining new insights is just one part of coaching. Real change doesn't happen until you apply what you've learned. We will show how to transform your inspirational moments into new behavior patterns and actions that impact your daily life, helping you go from theoretical to actual with ease.

And So Much More!

Throughout this work, we reference our own experiences with clients as well as those of other coaches to highlight and exemplify the methods and practices discussed in this book. Some of their names have been changed to protect their identities (and maybe even the innocent!).

Thank you for joining us on this incredible journey and allowing us to help you get the most out of coaching. We are honored to have you with us, and we look forward to helping you achieve greater personal fulfillment and experience immediate, life-changing results.

"Every famous athlete, every famous performer has somebody who is a coach, somebody ... who can give them outside perspective. The one thing that people are never good at is seeing themselves as others see them."[1]

—Eric Schmidt, Former CEO and Chairman of Google

---

1 Ravi Raman, "Eric Schmidt on Why 'Everybody Needs a Coach,'" Medium, https://medium.com/@yogiravi/eric-schmidt-says-everybody-needs-a-coach-8b0bd3f5f28b.

CHAPTER 1

THE IMPACT OF COACHING

D
r. Atul Gawande is a well-respected surgeon, public health professor, and writer. He entered into medical practice in 2003, and for several years, he experienced a steady trend of learning and improving. The rates of complications for his patients continually dropped over the course of five years, but he was surprised to see it level out after that. In fact, after five years of honing his skills, he didn't seem to be getting any better at all, despite having far more experience. He wondered if he was as good a surgeon as he would ever be.

As part of his work writing for the *New Yorker*, Gawande had done research on working with coaches. He learned that many professionals relied on coaches to help them identify their blind spots and suggest improvements they wouldn't have been able to pinpoint on their own. He thought he might benefit from working with a coach, so he decided to give it a shot. Gawande called up Dr. Bob Osteen, a retired former professor of his, who agreed to come to Gawande's operating room and observe him.

Gawande vividly remembers the first time being under observation, and was happy that the surgery went beautifully. He was confident that Osteen wouldn't have much to coach him on, since everything went so smoothly. You can imagine his surprise when he saw that Osteen had a full page of densely packed notes. "Just small things," Osteen said. "But it's the small things that matter."

Osteen went on to share a wide range of observations with Gawande. For example, the lighting wasn't positioned as well as it could have been to see the patient, which put everyone at an unnecessary disadvantage. He also noticed that Gawande's elbow was too high at times, showing he wasn't fully in control. Osteen advised Gawande to choose a different instrument when he felt his elbow begin to rise, or to simply take a small step to the side to get a better angle.

"It was a whole other level of awareness," said Gawande. He realized he had immediately tapped into the power of working with a great coach. He explained that Osteen essentially served as another, more-objective set of eyes and ears, providing him with a more-accurate picture of his reality. "I had to think," he said. "There was something fundamentally profound about this."

Within two months, Gawande felt himself improving again after a long and frustrating plateau. And that year, his rate of complications in surgery decreased.

But that wasn't the end of his coaching journey. Gawande was so impressed by his personal results that he decided to implement coaching at his other job at Ariadne Labs, a company focused on improving the delivery of healthcare—specifically for childbirth globally. The company partnered with the World Health Organization to create a safe childbirth checklist to help medical teams understand critical actions during labor and delivery, such as washing hands, using clean equipment, and monitoring blood pressure—common safety practices many medical teams in developing countries were not following.

Ariadne Labs implemented a coaching practice in a region of India and in Namibia, where infants and mothers needed it most. They partnered with a team of coaches to work with hundreds of doctors, nurses, and managers to not only follow the safe childbirth checklist but to build on their strengths and improve on their weaknesses. The coaches regularly visited the birthing centers for months, observing the medical teams and providing feedback.

One of the most common opportunities for improvement was communication. The coaches found that the teams knew they were supposed to be using sterile equipment, but the nurses didn't always feel comfortable speaking up when they ran out of clean gloves or other supplies. With regular coaching, the culture shifted, and the results were astonishing. Compliance with the checklist went up dramatically, leading to better patient outcomes.

On one occasion, Gawande got to personally watch nurses in India step into action when a baby was born not breathing. They quickly went through their checklist, as they had been coached to do, and used manual suction to clear out the baby's airways. Within a few minutes, she started to breathe.[1] This was just one life saved among many. Over the course of six months in Namibia, the combined number of stillbirths and newborn deaths within the first week of life, known as perinatal mortality, dropped from 22 to 13.8 deaths per 1,000 deliveries.[2]

From medical professionals to corporate executives to elite musicians, the impact of coaching has been seen across industries, professions, and far-flung corners of the world. If you've recently hired a coach or you're still considering coaching, you might be wondering what you can expect. Will coaching actually work for you? And how will a coach be able to pinpoint exactly what would help you the most?

---

1 Atul Gawande, "Want to get great at something?
Get a coach," TED2017, https://www.ted.com/talks/
atul_gawande_want_to_get_great_at_something_get_a_coach?language=en#t-935291.
2 "The BetterBirth Study," Ariadne Labs, https://www.ariadnelabs.org/areas-of-work/
better-birth/.

You can take comfort in knowing that coaching works because of some simple truths about being human. We all have inner wisdom we can tap into when it comes to improving any area of our lives, but we become stuck in seeing things from a certain viewpoint. As Gawande discovered, sometimes it can be impossible to effectively identify the beliefs or actions that are holding us back. Working with a coach is like getting a bonus set of eyes and ears. They help us break down our actions, see things from a different perspective, and consider new possibilities. Coaches serve as a catalyst for accelerating our learning and better connecting with our inner wisdom.

Coaching is a fierce art—not a science. Great coaches draw from their intuition and inherent creativity to help clients find success, personal growth, and fulfillment in order to get to the heart of what it means to be human.

Perhaps Julio Olalla, one of the early pioneers of coaching and the ontological approach, said it best: "It is about wisdom and having a love affair with questions. Knowledge is a love affair with answers. We are so attracted by knowledge—we measure it, possess it, patent it—that we've lost concern for wisdom."[3]

A coach coming from a place of wisdom has a natural curiosity, which stimulates questions and opens new doorways for their clients. These questions don't necessarily need to be answered. Instead, they offer guidance, pointing to a "way of being" that shifts your perception of the circumstances surrounding you and leads you to different actions and better results.

Great coaches take a powerful, multidimensional approach aimed at unlocking deep issues that may block you from moving forward. Your sessions will examine the complex interrelationships between language, listening, speaking, emotions, physiological

---

[3] Julio Olalla, "Amo La Vida," Newfield Network, 7:00, https://www.youtube.com/watch?v=1tBWnwghi8E.

states, and more to provide a richer, deeper understanding of how to move your life forward. It's an enlightening, enjoyable, and rewarding experience.

Our best advice is to find a coach you trust and go all in. Be humble, let go of preconceived notions, and make a conscious choice that you will be coachable. If you commit to learning, growing, and following the best practices in this book, we truly believe the impact that you see in your life from coaching will amaze you.

"You must expect great
things of yourself before
you can do them."

—Michael Jordan

CHAPTER 2

DEFINING YOUR COACHING GOALS

N ow that you understand the benefits of coaching, you may be wondering what kinds of results you can expect. If you were to commit to the process now, what would your life be like in three months? What about in a year, or five years? We wish it were possible to provide specific answers to your deepest, burning questions, but the reality is that your results from coaching truly depend on you, what you want to achieve, and your commitment to the overall coaching process.

What would give you the greatest returns from coaching? Would you want to get promoted, double your company's revenue, or sell the business you built and earn a huge profit? Maybe you'd want to rekindle the romance in your marriage, build a better relationship with your kids, or stop sweating the little things and be more content in the present moment? When it comes to coaching, our clients have achieved all of these goals, and we've seen firsthand how anything is possible.

Your coach will work with you and support you in going after whatever kind of growth or achievement you desire, but it's important to know that there are different ways to think about personal transformation. Drs. Ron and Mary Hulnick, coauthors of the book *Remembering the Light Within*, are pioneers and worldwide leaders in Spiritual Psychology and Leadership at the University of Santa Monica, and have created a model for understanding our spiritual and achievement-oriented realities of the physical world by dividing them into two categories:

LOVE

Spiritual Reality
(The Soul Line)

(-)   (+)

Physical World Reality
(The Goal Line)

Soul Line: This kind of transformation focuses on inner growth, such as becoming more mindful and cultivating a greater sense of inner peace. These kinds of goals are harder to measure, and the path for making progress might be less straightforward than with achievement-based goals.

Goal Line: When you have outward, measurable achievements that you want to home in on during coaching, such as increasing your earnings by $100K in a single year, you're targeting a goal-line transformation. If you have a corporate sponsor that is paying for coaching, you can probably expect to go this route, as businesses tend to be serious about goal setting, measurement, and accountability.

Karen's former coach, Steve Chandler, often shares the story of his coach, Steve Hardison, being approached by a CEO of a company that had made $500M in revenue. The CEO told Steve that he wanted to take his company to a billion dollars in revenue and asked Steve if he could help him do it. Steve's response was that he could indeed help create the man who could create a company that made a billion in revenue. In other words, Steve would work on who this CEO was *being* as he worked to create the growth and expansion of his organization he was hoping to achieve. This is a great example of Soul Line coaching.

Although Soul Line and Goal Line transformation are different, we often recommend taking a hybrid approach. That's because your Soul Line is so intertwined with your Goal Line that when you work on one, you're often also working on the other. For example, if you want to get promoted, you must first become a better leader. There's a lot of necessary inner work that needs to be done before that outward goal becomes realistic. You might need to work on being more compassionate and authentic so that you earn the trust of your colleagues. When you make that progress, you naturally get closer to getting that promotion. As you begin to embody a new way of being and rise up the Soul Line, your outer achievement-oriented Goal Line also rises. This is a holistic way of looking at personal development.

What Do You Want Most?

Before a coach can support you in any kind of transformation, you need to figure out what's most important to you. Sometimes this is easier said than done. We urge you to dig deep and be honest with yourself and your coach—even if it feels like baring your soul. Otherwise, you might find yourself making good time but going in the wrong direction.

Steve Chandler shares a parable of a man who tells his coach that he wants to create a rocket to fly to the moon. The coach says, "Great!" so they start working on building the rocket. After several months of hard work, the coach finally asks the man why he was so inspired to create the rocket. "So I can get away from my wife!" he says. "She's driving me crazy!" The coach is shocked. Why hadn't the man just said he needed to work on his relationship with his wife? That would have been a lot easier and more straightforward than trying to get him to the moon on a homemade rocket! This is a lighthearted example, but it makes a serious point: Establishing the right intentions up front saves time and energy down the road.

It's important to note that many coaches gravitate toward a certain type of approach in their sessions. Some coaches are very meticulous about following a plan and focusing on goals, whereas others prefer to be in the moment with coaching and work on whatever comes up organically in sessions. Neither approach is right or wrong, but it's definitely possible that one is better suited to your individual interests or needs. With this in mind, make sure you speak up if you have a preference in the approach you want your coach to take. For example, if you thrive on structure, let your coach know.

Going deeper with your goals is the best way to affect change in your life. The most meaningful goals we could set for ourselves might not be the ones we inherently gravitate toward. That's because our deepest desires aren't always hanging out on the surface. Sometimes even the act of acknowledging that we want certain things can be a struggle. It makes us vulnerable to admit—even to ourselves—that we desire something different from what we've worked toward, or what others might expect of us. It's also difficult to admit when we want something more, especially if there's no guarantee that we'll be able to get it. Going for more opens the door to success, but in the short term may also temporarily feel like failure.

Reflection Questions

The following exercise is meant to help you find clarity on what to focus on with your coach. Take some time to brainstorm the following questions, and write your answers in a notebook.

- Is there something missing from my life? If so, how am I keeping it out?
- What's not working for me in my lifestyle, career, or relationships?
- What are three things that I've been tolerating in these areas?
- Do I hold myself back in certain ways? How?
- Am I waiting for something to go away before I take action?
- What scares me? Why?
- What is the hardest thing in my life that I've had to overcome? How has it made me stronger?
- What is my truest intention?
- If I knew I couldn't fail, what would I most want to have, or accomplish?
- What am I really committed to, and what am I doing to show my commitment?

After you've brainstormed these questions, think about how you could leverage this information in your coaching sessions. Your coach will probably work with you in the first few sessions to establish a sense of direction and understand what success looks like for you when it comes to coaching. However, collectively, you may not immediately hit on all the questions that hold your most important answers. Make sure you give your coach an honest, big-picture view of what your life is like and what matters most to you. If that little voice in the back of your head is telling you to speak up about something, do it. The more your coach knows about you, the more they can support you. Being transparent will only be a benefit in this situation.

Executive Sponsorship

Companies often invest in hiring coaches for their leaders. There are various scenarios when this happens. In some cases, once you reach a certain level at a company, it becomes a requirement—or a benefit, depending on your perspective! In other cases, a company will bring coaches in to help a leader get through a challenging situation, prepare for a specific role, or simply boost their performance. In each of these situations, the company is invested in their employee's success, and they recognize the value in getting personalized support from a third party.

If your company is footing the bill for coaching, you will most likely work with your manager and your coach at the beginning of the engagement to define your goals. If your manager isn't that hands-on, chances are they will at least review a plan that you put together with your coach. In either case, your goals will be focused on your professional role, since that's what your manager wants to see, and what your company is paying for.

When you're in this kind of coaching relationship with an executive sponsor, it could be easy for you to assume that personal matters are off-limits. Luckily, that usually is not the case. Boundaries between work and personal life can be difficult to define, especially when it comes to your headspace. If you're going through a personal challenge that's requiring a lot of mental bandwidth, it will keep you from focusing on your job. That's exactly the kind of thing your coach needs to know about to provide you the best possible support.

Karen frequently coaches leaders who have executive sponsors, and is passionate about providing whole-person support. In fact, on the few occasions when companies have asked her to focus only on the professional side of coaching rather than addressing anything on a personal level, Karen has told them that she can't effectively do her job without providing a holistic approach.

Every coach is different, so if you're in an executive-sponsorship relationship, make sure you ask your coach if there are any boundaries when it comes to supporting you on your personal growth.

Develop a Road Map

Have you ever sought to achieve a personal goal but fell short? We all have! Whether it's wanting to eat healthier, keep in closer touch with friends, or revamp our business websites, wanting to do something and actually doing it are two totally different things. One reason these kinds of goals fall through the cracks is they don't have a plan supporting them. Another reason is it's easy to lose sight of how great it would be to achieve these goals. To help with both of these issues, we recommend creating a road map for your goals that focuses on intentions, commitments, and benefits. When you can identify these key aspects of your goals, it's much easier to work with your coach and focus on what matters most.

Karen recently worked with a client who has had an incredible amount of success creating a road map of her goals. Jen was primarily focused on her professional growth—that is, until she was diagnosed with Lyme disease and had to get serious about her health. She had been experiencing a range of symptoms that had worsened over many years, and before she knew it, even getting out of bed was a challenge. Before Jen could dig into the professional goals she'd set for herself, she needed to reassess her priorities to focus on health.

There are many methods for treating Lyme, and most of them require substantial amounts of time, money, energy, and focus. Karen worked with Jen to set specific goals around the many things health professionals had advised her to do. Since it all added up to quite a bit of extra work that Jen wasn't particularly excited about doing, she had to stay focused on the benefits of her efforts in order to keep herself motivated.

The following chart is an example (using Jen) of a goal-setting tool we use with our clients. You can see Jen identified "Health" as one of her priorities, what she committed to doing, and how it would help her and her family. Clients typically pick between four and five themes they want to focus on for improvement, such as health, work, relationships, finances, spiritual, work impact, or special projects. Using present tense, they fill in their top intentions, the commitments they will make, and the benefits that will come from their achievements—for themselves and others. Your brain will naturally respond to messages in the present rather than in the past or future tense. Thinking about how your efforts will benefit those around you adds another layer of motivation, making this tool even more powerful.

It is important to understand the distinction between intentions and commitments. Intentions are those initiatives that you would like to create in your life and follow. Commitments are precise and measurable actions that you are 100 percent going to do. We recommend going through the road map process once a year to adjust your intentions and commitments as things change in your life. We've seen how our clients' goals evolve over time as they grow and learn more about themselves—and it's been rewarding to see them continue to take their coaching insights to the next level.

Jen's Road Map (Partial Example)

Health: My health is a top priority for me this year. The Lyme is in remission and I feel super strong and pain-free. I am grateful to be in remission. I am highly conscious of what I eat. I am getting stronger every day and taking very good care of my body.

Intentions	Commitments	Benefits
I am taking my medications and following doctor(s) orders	• I set alarms on my phone • I am doing intermittent fasting 5 days a week • I'm drinking Superfood Smoothies 5 days a week • I drink alcohol ONLY on rare occasions • I limit my sugar intake • I drink more water than I think I need • I am getting all my preventative-care shots • I am listening to my body's wisdom • I am financially investing in my health, without question • I am in flow, grace, and ease	• I am learning how powerful I am • I am experiencing energy, vitality, and creativity • I have less body pain • My thinking is clear • My family experiences me as fully present and able to take part in activities • My family worries less about my health • I can better serve my organization and clients
I am exercising	• I am walking every day • I am enjoying yoga 2X a week • I am strength training 5X a week for 30 minutes each morning	• I feel good about the way I feel • My clothes are no longer tight • I am enjoying skiing and hiking
I am meditating	• I sit for 10 minutes each day • I set a timer • I record my meditation in my diary	• My mind is at peace • I am more present with my family

Whatever format you and your coach decide to use for tracking your goals, this document will serve as your North Star as you embark on the coaching journey. Whenever you feel a little lost or unsure of where to focus, come back to your goals. Ask yourself whether you're following through with what you planned on doing, or if you've veered off track.

Don't forget to give yourself grace. Change can take time and hard work. Be patient with yourself and know that your coach is on your side and your efforts will indeed pay off.

Carefully identifying your coaching goals is a critical foundational step toward success. After all, if you haven't decided where you want to go yet, how can you possibly know when you get there?

Coachability is a set of
traits and habits that
enable you to make all
your goals and dreams
come true.

CHAPTER 3

IMPROVING YOUR COACHABILITY

You wouldn't have picked up this book in the first place if you weren't interested in improving yourself and your life. And while you want to find a truly awesome coach to accompany you on this journey, there is someone who's infinitely more important in this process: You. Simply put, the more coachable you can be, the more you will achieve and the faster you will grow.

What do we mean by "coachability"? Coachability is a set of traits and habits that enable you to make all your goals and dreams come true. Since you and your coach will work on developing those characteristics together, you won't necessarily have them all from the get-go. But it's good to have an understanding of what will make you become more coachable—so the work you put in can actually work.

It's important to note that these traits are not requirements for working with a coach. In fact, very few individuals are strong in all of these areas—top performers included. As coaches, we hope to find people who have strength in a couple of these areas. This gives a solid foundation to start making improvements. As we work with our clients and they grow over time, our sessions help awaken other coachability traits that were lying dormant, while also teaching the skills for using those traits effectively.

As you read the following, take some mental notes on the traits that resonate with you most, as well as those that could be areas for improvement.

Coachability Traits and Tenets

Action Oriented

There can be no transformation without action between coaching sessions. That's why this is the single-most-important factor in coachability. The people who gain the most from coaching are those with a growth mindset that fuels them to take immediate action. After coaching sessions, they do something differently right away. By tackling challenges and opportunities quickly, they can ultimately cover a lot more ground with coaching than can those who do not have a bias for action.

Willingness to Accept Guidance

This seems like an obvious one, but sometimes your ego gets in the way of you being receptive to guidance and feedback. Deep down, we want to change, but our mind doesn't want to accept that we need to do anything differently. That's why our initial reaction to any kind of advice or suggestion can sometimes be rejection (e.g., "That's never going to work. If I took that approach to resolve the issue, it would just be a waste of time.").

Your coach's job is to help disrupt the status quo and give you a new perspective, so expect to be presented with guidance you hadn't previously considered. Your job is to fall out of your ego and lead with your heart. Be humble and accept that there may be better ways of doing things than how you've done them in the past. This will require you to monitor the voices in your head and keep them firmly in check. In fact, you just might want to keep your thumb on the mute button. If you are open to new ideas and you give them a real chance, you might be surprised at how impactful they could be in your life.

Openness to Experimentation and Testing

The people who get the most out of coaching are open to diving in and trying new things in order to see what works. For example, one of Alex's clients was having trouble making progress on her goals because she was uncomfortable with ambiguity. She wanted to control all the details and have the perfect premeditated outcome for all her projects before starting them. In other words, she was constantly experiencing paralysis by analysis.

Alex suggested she experiment with taking an improv class as an interesting way to introduce flexibility into her life. At first, she hated the idea but signed up for an improv class anyway, and ended up loving it so much that she's still taking classes years later! It also worked wonders on her incessant need to plan and control everything in her life. Today, she's much more willing and able to go with the flow, which has enabled her to take her career to the next level.

Your coach's job is to shake up your thinking and steer you away from your default path and toward your created path. Remaining open to experimentation and testing will speed up that process because you won't have to keep battling your own resistance to new ideas. When your coach suggests that you try something different, you can experiment with it immediately rather than weigh the options in your mind for weeks while you assess whether it's worth trying. This kind of positive mindset will ultimately lead to totally different results because you're able to accomplish so much more both in your sessions and outside of them.

Self-Awareness

Truly understanding yourself and your behavior patterns can be difficult. It takes time and effort to listen to your thoughts, observe how you interact, and think about what it all means. Some people are naturally more introspective than others, but everyone can boost their self-awareness in a variety of ways, including therapy, personal development work, personality assessment tools, and of course, coaching. As you become more self-aware, your coachability will increase because you'll have a better understanding of how your thoughts, words, and actions impact the people around you—and you'll be able to go deeper faster with your coach.

Strong Opinions

Your coach's goal is never to push you in a direction you do not want to go. Instead, they want to help you reach the goals you set for yourself and get there in a way that works for you. With that in mind, coachability should not be confused with being blindly subservient to everything your coach has to say. While the monastery where Alex trained was, fittingly, on a hill, coaches are not all-powerful gurus. As a matter of fact, it's actually against ICF's core competencies for a coach to lead a client or give advice without specific permission from that client.

Coaches are trained to listen, ask open-ended questions to evoke your inner wisdom, and seek permission from you before offering advice that might help. Whatever they say is by no means an order. If you disagree with a recommendation, it's best to be honest and let your coach know that the suggestion just isn't resonating with you. This is helpful feedback for your coach, and it will allow them to better serve you.

Curiosity

Having an interest in learning and trying new things translates well to coaching. This curiosity will help you remain open to new ideas and excited about doing things differently. One way of considering this aspect of coachability is to imagine the world through a child's eyes, where everything is new, thrilling, and worthy of exploration. Children don't have preconceived notions about the world only working in certain ways, and they aren't stuck in old patterns of thinking that no longer serve them. They have room for new ideas, and they embrace them wholeheartedly. This kind of mindset is ideal for coaching; be open and empty so you can receive. Since this will enable you to make quick progress on your goals, don't ever be afraid to let your inner child out to play.

Optimistic

In the face of a setback or disappointment, people want the ability to recover and claim a happy state of mind. Some are hardwired to excel at this, while others can learn it by adopting a positive framework during adverse conditions. It's important to note that coaching can create periods of discomfort as you stretch and grow—it's an innate part of the process. If you can keep an optimistic outlook, you'll be better able to sustain your happiness while you work toward your goals.

Sense of Humor

We've been coaches for many years. We actually met in a coaching program organized by our aforementioned coach, Steve Chandler. One reason we both loved working with Steve is his sense of humor. He's like a stand-up comedian when he gets in front of a group of people, which makes the learning process so much more fun and interesting. We both have fond memories of being in a group session in which one of the students brought in a stuffed dolphin and a plastic Wiffle ball bat as a funny way to riff with Steve on one of his teaching points from a few weeks prior. He had said that in order to train a dolphin you teach it by rewarding it, not abusing it—drawing the connection to how to treat clients. Steve loved it and began playing out a little scene for our group in which he smacked the stuffed dolphin around with the Wiffle ball bat while repeating, "You don't... want... to treat them... like... this." People were almost in tears from laughing so hard!

Just because you're focusing on important aspects of your life doesn't mean that your sessions have to take on a feeling of heaviness. You can absolutely keep it light and humorous. Don't be afraid to poke fun at yourself, joke with your coach, or take a jovial approach to your sessions. This will help you stay motivated and look forward to conversations with your coach.

Integrity

Your word is everything. It's how you show people you're trustworthy and reliable. Showing up for your sessions on time and prepared is you being true to your word, to yourself. If you have a bad habit of being late, coaching will be an opportunity for you to get that habit cleaned up once and for all in every aspect of your life.

Karen had a client who was a busy executive, going from meeting to meeting. He thought it was impossible for him to arrive on time for his sessions. When Karen asked him if he'd ever missed an airline flight, he said, "No," with a sense of great pride.

Karen said, "Great, let's treat your coaching time like you are catching a flight." From that day forward, he was never late for a session (although he did ask for a tiny bag of pretzels on occasion!).

Being a person of integrity who is on time slowly expanded to other areas of his life because of the coaching.

In coaching, honesty and integrity are incredibly important in helping your coach understand what's going on in your life. If you make a mistake or have a part in creating a messy situation, you need to step up to fix things. If you weren't able to follow through with whatever you said you were going to do, your coach needs to know. Hiding that information could damage your coach's ability to work with you effectively. We often tell our clients, "If you mess up, fess up," as encouragement to speak up if they need to admit something. This helps us keep the lines of communication open so we can make progress.

Commitment to the Process

Doing what you say you're going to do seems like a simple thing, but we know that's not always the case. Life gets busy, priorities shift, and plans get put on the back burner. But if you really want coaching to change your life, committing to the process—and your action items—is essential. Sometimes this level of dedication can feel overwhelming, especially to those who are new to coaching.

One way to think about it is by considering the areas of your life where you are already committed to showing up no matter what. Even if it's something small, such as walking your dog three times a day or never missing your monthly leadership meeting, it's easy to see that you are reliable and dedicated in certain areas of your life. If you can do it there, you can do it elsewhere. Sometimes it takes a "come to Jesus" moment for you to realize you need to make a change.

We've seen people experience this at many different phases of coaching, from before they start having sessions to months or even years in. It can be a difficult transformation, but we truly believe that once 10 percent of a person makes a decision to change, 90 percent of the universe gets behind that person and their decision.[1]

Summary

The purpose of coaching is to assist you in making important transformations in your life. The types of changes are totally up to you, but the goal is to gain insights that allow you to unlock the growth you've been seeking. If you aren't willing to accept guidance, take action, commit, and employ the other coachability traits highlighted in this chapter, you will continue on your default path, rather than your chosen path. That's why it's so important to focus on enhancing these traits over time. Start by leaning on your strengths. As you work with your coach, you will see more of these skills emerge in the way you think and show up.

Coaching is not a linear journey in which you simply go from point A to point B. It's a meandering path that takes a good deal of time to travel. Even if you're excited about making progress, remember that patience is key. Take a moment to slow down, center yourself, and practice gratitude that you've come this far. Instead of worrying that you haven't achieved "perfect coachability" (which isn't actually a thing), treat yourself with love and kindness. We're all on our own journey, and the thing that matters most is not giving up.

Particularly if you're new to this process, your best "ability" is "coachability." So revisiting these tenets to make sure you're giving yourself the very best chance to succeed is never a bad idea.

---

1 Paraphrased from Gary Zukov's *The Seat of the Soul.*

"Clear is kind."

—Brené Brown

CHAPTER 4

HOLDING NOTHING BACK

Another key way to make sure you get the most from your relationship with your coach is to hold nothing back yourself. Take the following prime example:

Years ago, Karen was working with Allison, a corporate executive at a multimillion-dollar company. The company was footing the bill for coaching, and Karen knew Allison had fired her last coach. She was eager to form a positive relationship with Allison, earn her trust, and help her achieve her goals. But after just a couple of sessions, Karen could tell that Allison had preconceived notions about coaching that were keeping her from opening up. Karen had a hunch she was holding back something big: that she might be having an affair with a colleague. If her intuition was correct, it was potentially a catastrophic issue, since it could potentially cause Allison to lose both her job and her marriage.

As Allison's coach, Karen felt compelled to help before her life came crashing down like a house of cards, but she didn't want to overstep any boundaries, especially with a new client who'd had trust issues with her past coach. After a couple more sessions, Allison finally opened up and told Karen that she was indeed having an affair with a work colleague. She was caught off guard by Karen's lack of surprise. Allison had held off telling her because she wasn't ready to end the affair or her marriage, and she didn't want to be judged. But when she finally opened up to Karen, she learned that coaches aren't in the business of passing judgment on their clients; they are simply there to help.

From that moment on, Karen was able to offer Allison the support she needed. Allison chose to end the affair, be honest with her husband, and commit to couple's therapy. Karen helped find a talented therapist for Allison and her husband, and they were able to work through their issues. The affair never came to light at the company, and Allison was eventually promoted to CEO. Years later, her career is thriving and her relationship with her husband has never been better.

Just like Allison, we all have aspects of our lives that aren't perfect. We've also withheld our own share of sensitive information from our own coaches. It can be uncomfortable to talk about our indiscretions, mistakes, or the root causes of whatever is holding us back. But those are usually the areas where we need the most help.

Honest Conversations

Over the years, we've seen countless people struggle with opening up and having honest conversations that get to the heart of what's most important. Sometimes we can tell when there's a specific issue bubbling below the surface that clients don't want to discuss, but other times we just see that progress is moving slowly.

Our longtime coach and friend, Steve Chandler, has a technique of asking clients, "What's at the bottom of your discussion list today?" What he means is, "What's the last thing you feel like talking about with me today?" It's a question that makes us both laugh and cringe because it's spot-on for driving conversations that unlock personal growth. Quite often, the thing we least want to talk about is the area that needs the most attention. If you don't share this information, your coach can't help you.

We all have a tendency to subconsciously filter the information we share with others or tell white lies about how we're doing or the progress we've made. This behavior is baked into the social norms of our culture. We don't usually expect a fully honest answer, or even an answer at all, when we ask someone, "How are you?" Most of us aren't in the habit of baring our souls to strangers—or even friends. It's natural to safeguard the stories, problems, and desires that could cause others to judge us, but when it comes to coaching, we need to take a fresh approach and hold nothing back. Vulnerability is paramount.

One thing that can help you open up during your sessions is remembering that, unlike certain friends or family members, your coach is not attached to you achieving a certain outcome. Rather than pushing you in a specific direction, a coach evokes your inner wisdom about choosing your own path. This is an important distinction because it means that your coach will never be disappointed by your choices—or make you feel inadequate or bad about yourself. Instead of creating expectations for you, your coach is your best advocate working to help you achieve the goals you have set for yourself. That's why it pays off to be honest with your coach from the start.

Being transparent often requires intentionality. You have to get into a different mindset than the one you have in typical social relationships. There should be no motivation to come across as likeable, charming, or impressive to your coach; they just want to see the real you—imperfections and all. If it takes time to open up, that's okay. Very few people are able to be fully transparent in the first session or two, or maybe even longer.

Reflection Questions

Vulnerability starts with self-awareness. Ask yourself the following questions to assess your own level of openness and vulnerability.

- On a scale of 1–10 (1 being "not at all" and 10 being "extremely"), how open and vulnerable do I feel with my coach?
- What made me choose that number instead of something lower?
- What do I find difficult to talk about?
- What would make it easier for me to open up?
- What kind of agreements would I need to make with my coach in order to feel more open and vulnerable?
- Who am I most open and vulnerable with? What is it about them that makes it easier?
- When something upsets me, do I have trouble talking about it?
- When I talk with friends or family, do I tend to downplay certain emotions or experiences?
- Do I have secret's I've never told anyone?
- If something is weighing on my mind, how do I typically work through it?
- What is the one thing I don't want my coach to know about me?

Being vulnerable is an ongoing journey rather than a destination. Even if you're an open book today, that might shift in the coming months as issues get resolved in your sessions. When you notice yourself holding back from sharing key information with your coach, make it a habit to "tell on yourself." It is your responsibility to bring up every issue. While coaches can draw upon experience to suss out issues beneath the surface, they are not psychics. Just like working with a personal trainer and speaking up when your knee starts hurting, you have to learn to be your own advocate. Your coach is going to train you differently if they know about the pain. If you don't speak up, it reduces their ability to meet your needs, which can jeopardize your results.

Giving Feedback

Along the same lines, you should feel empowered to give your coach feedback in real time during your sessions. If you're hoping for more insight on a specific topic, say so. If a perspective or suggestion they shared with you just isn't resonating, be honest and voice your concerns. This kind of forthright, two-way communication is the most effective way to make progress toward your goals.

If you're working with a therapist or spiritual advisor, or you're practicing a specific personal-growth modality, make sure to let your coach know that, too. It is important to make sure coaching aligns with and complements what you're already doing. One of Karen's clients once said, "Therapy is about recovery, and coaching is about discovery." This is an excellent example of how multiple growth practices can dovetail and support one another on your journey.

Don't Take Things Personally

A few years ago, Karen began coaching Dave, a middle manager working in the insurance industry. Dave's primary goal was to get promoted at his company, and he was bitter that it was taking him so many years to climb the corporate ladder. Several of his colleagues had been promoted over him or head-hunted for higher-ranking positions at other companies. Karen typically coaches executives rather than middle managers, but Dave took that as a sign that Karen could help him reach his goal of obtaining an executive position.

Right off the bat, Karen enjoyed working with Dave. He was driven and motivated, and she could see that he would make meaningful progress quickly. She even told Alex how excited she was to be coaching her new client.

But something strange happened in the third session. Dave showed up with a hostile attitude. Within the first couple minutes, he blurted out, "If I'm not the type of client you're used to working with and you don't want to work with me, it's okay."

Karen was taken aback. She told Dave that she was excited to be working with him and asked if she had done something to make him think otherwise. It all came pouring out that on the last call, Dave heard Karen make an "exasperated sound" at the end of their coaching session. Dave assumed Karen was annoyed with him and frustrated about his lack of professional success, and no longer wanted to work with him.

At first, Karen didn't know what he was talking about. She certainly didn't feel that way about him, and had no idea what sound she could have possibly uttered that would cause him to question her devotion to their coaching relationship. But then she remembered that at the end of their previous call her attention had drifted to the additional personality assessment she impulsively threw in during the session at no additional fee. It was an assessment she felt would be very important for Dave, but was not part of the original scope of work. Karen suddenly remembered she would need to pay a third-party expert for the assessment, and the exasperated sound she made was directed at herself for not having the foresight to build it into the contract. (Going above and beyond the scope of client contracts is something she's done many times in the past, and she's happy to do it, but paying third-party fees is a bummer.)

She explained this all to Dave and told him that the sigh was in no way directed at him, and that she was on his side. He was skeptical of her story, which struck Karen as a red flag. Why was he so sure that she must not want to work with him?

This ended up sparking a highly productive conversation. Dave shared that he carried a constant feeling of inadequacy for being stuck in the same role at his company for so long. He felt like everyone in his life thought deep down that he was a loser. They all knew why he hadn't been promoted; it was because he wasn't good enough, smart enough, or talented enough. He confessed that he was shy about reaching out to Karen because she specializes in coaching executives, and he was worried that she would think he was a loser too, inferior to her other clients. Karen and Dave went on to create a highly impactful coaching relationship, and Dave was promoted to the executive ranks.

When you're sensitive about a particular issue in your life, and you consider it a shortcoming, it's easy to believe that other people are constantly judging you for it. If you're concerned about the 15 pounds you've recently gained, you might worry that other people think you're fat. It's likely that no one has noticed, let alone judged you for it, but the voices in your head can take over and give you an inferiority complex. When that happens, it's very easy to take offense to things that were not at all meant as criticisms. For example, your friend gets you a new sweater for your birthday, and you notice the tag reads XL. If you're sensitive about your weight, the size could ruin the gift for you, even if you like the sweater and it fits perfectly. All you see is that your friend thinks you're big, and they're right.

Living with this point of view is painful and emotionally draining. That's why Dave was so quick to lash out at Karen when he thought she was judging him. To Dave, her behavior wasn't an anomaly that called for a question like, "Did I say something you don't agree with?" Instead, he just assumed the worst, which happened to be way off base.

It's important to realize when you're feeling sensitive about certain areas of your life and recognize when you're reading too much into other people's words or actions. This comes up a lot in coaching, both in the relationship you have with your coach and the relationships you have with other people. You'll be pushing yourself and stretching in new ways, and you might get feedback that bothers you or makes you feel defensive. When this happens, you need to do your best to remain open instead of closing up. That's how you'll make real progress.

Reflection

When you're sensitive about something, an annoying little voice in the back of your head tells you that you aren't good enough. Author Brené Brown calls these voices "shame gremlins" because, just like the characters from the movie *Gremlins*, these voices can be like evil monsters. They say things like, "You are not smart enough. You are not pretty enough. You are not worthy. Your spouse left you because you are worthless. You never get the promotion because you have no skills."[1]

To conquer shame gremlins, you must first learn to recognize them. To get started, read through the following list of topics that commonly cause people to feel inadequate.

- Likeability
- Social status
- Professional status
- Work history

[1] https://medium.com/monday-motivator/the-shame-gremlin-c60001596e69 accessed 1-15-20

- Intelligence
- Socioeconomic status/background
- Body size/shape
- Education
- Relationship/family status
- Race/ethnicity
- Gender

Do any of these strike a chord with you? Take a moment and sit with that feeling.

As you think about holding nothing back, make sure you release the negative, limiting beliefs and shame gremlins—you won't need any of them where you're going.

When you take it all into consideration, facing everything and holding nothing back is one of the best ways for you to ensure that you can keep consistently moving forward.

Before each session, ask yourself, "If I could only work on one thing, what would it be?"

CHAPTER 5

MAKING THE MOST OF YOUR SESSIONS

L ife these days is moving at a million miles an hour. Consequently, we're all trying to juggle way too much. And to be brutally honest, "multitasking" is just another way of saying "I'm really not doing anything particularly well." That's why it is utterly essential that you are totally present and prepared for every one of your coaching sessions. Otherwise, you're just wasting both your time and your money. An anecdote from Alex's childhood is definitely relevant in this realm.

When Alex was younger, he and his brother loved the rock band KISS. They used to crank up the radio and play air guitar together all the time, but Andy wanted to learn how to play a real guitar. So, when Andy turned seven, their mother signed him up for a handful of introductory lessons at a musical instrument shop downtown.

The lessons were half an hour long. It wasn't worth dropping Andy off only to turn around and pick him back up again, so Andy's mom waited for him in the car while he went inside to meet with his instructor. She could see them through the front window sitting in the showroom amidst the guitars and drum kits. All seemed to be going well until she noticed that during the third and fourth lessons, Andy was missing for a good part of the time.

Before the fifth lesson began, she went into the store to meet with the teacher to ask what was going on. Why was he not getting taught how to play during the full half hour? The teacher said,

"Oh, he's asked to go to the bathroom a couple of times, so I'm letting him."

The teacher didn't recognize stalling, a simple tactic kids sometimes use to get out of doing things that end up being harder than they originally anticipated. Andy wanted to learn to play guitar, but in the moment, it seemed easier to take a little break.

Can you relate to how the resistance in this story works? You want to learn something. You want to change. You'll even make the effort to sign up for a class or hire a coach, and then you notice how it's not always fun or exciting. And it's certainly not easy. Part of you really wants things to be different while another part of you argues for things to stay the same. Can you hear your thoughts? "My situation isn't so bad. This might not work. I don't need one more thing on my plate. I can't afford this right now. Maybe I can do this on my own."

And if your thoughts don't create outright resistance, such as missing sessions or taking purported "bathroom breaks," it could be an even more subtle version of resistance, such as not bringing up the most important issue you face, or derailing the session in some way that waters it down and ensures you don't get what you're paying for. Perhaps most people don't blow all their session time in the restroom, but they find plenty of other ways to slow, stall, prevent, or outright sabotage their progress.

It's innocent. It's normal. It's even part of the process. But just because it's normal doesn't mean you have to go along with it. Instead, you can prepare yourself to face it.

When it comes to change, we all have complex and competing emotions. Part of us desperately wants to go through a transformation, while another part is invested in staying the same. We see the benefits of change, but we also see the ease and comfort in maintaining the status quo. Most people are actively trying to get the most out of coaching, but coaches may not be able to recognize all the ways that sessions can get derailed, which makes this self-sabotaging behavior especially problematic.

This chapter will help you understand the various ways you can derail a session and inadvertently prevent yourself from getting the most out of your sessions. When you know what to watch out for, it will be much easier to nip any problematic tendencies in the proverbial bud.

Derailments

Derailment #1: Not Being Prepared

One of the biggest issues that will hinder your coaching progress is not being prepared. Prior to your sessions, create a system for tracking what you want to work on with your coach. Make sure you have an answer when your coach asks you, "What is the highest value dream or challenge we can work on today?"

Though you want to come in open to what unfolds in the session, it's always important to be responsible for the direction you would like the session to go. Between sessions, think about what you want to work on with your coach. If you have a road map like we talked about in Chapter 2, ask yourself, "How does this issue or topic align with my road map?" Sometimes it won't, and that's fine as long as you are being conscious about your choices.

Tips for Avoiding This Derailment

Keep a list of what you want to talk about with your coach. Karen's system is to keep a "bring it to coach" list. She uses this list to keep track of topics on her phone using her Reminder app. That way, she always has a running list of what came up between sessions. She might happen to be on vacation walking along the beach, but if she thinks about a topic that would be great to discuss with her coach, she'll jot it down quickly so she doesn't forget it. Prior to her coaching session, she'll review what she jotted down previously and then pull out her coaching journal to prioritize certain topics and expand her thinking before her session. Create a system that works for you to ensure you always come prepared for your sessions.

Derailment #2: Avoiding the Real Issue

You may know deep down what your biggest challenge is, but you have a hard time tackling it head on. This can be for a variety of reasons, but it usually comes down to the fact that real transformation is hard work. It's uncomfortable to take a hard look at problematic areas of your life and admit that things are not going as well as you want. It's even more difficult to take the first steps toward real progress when you know there's a chance you might not succeed right away. But if you dance around the issue that would make the biggest transformation in your success, you are absolutely doing yourself—and your coach—a disservice.

Tips for Avoiding This Derailment

Ask yourself, "What do I not want my coach to know?" The answer could likely be the issue you need to discuss most. Have courage! Give yourself a pep talk, meditate, or do whatever you need to do to give your bravery a boost. Your coach is rooting for you and has your back 100 percent. Remember that you didn't sign up for coaching to derive pleasure from your sessions. Comfort is the enemy of growth.

Derailment #3: Focusing on Others

Coaching sessions can easily turn into gripe-and-moan sessions. Clients will often complain about all the people they view as being difficult, unreasonable, or otherwise hard to deal with. But it's impossible for coaches to change other people's behaviors because they are not in the room. The author of *The Advice Trap*, Michael Bungay Stanier, refers to this as "coaching the ghost." They haven't agreed to be coached, and they may have zero interest in changing any aspect of their behavior anyway. That's why it's generally unproductive to discuss other people's problems during your coaching sessions.

Tips for Avoiding This Derailment

If you find yourself in a ghost situation, ask yourself, "What's difficult here for me?" Or, "What's my responsibility in creating this?" Better yet, download the free "Judge Your Neighbor" worksheet from *The Work* by Byron Katie to help you process your emotions. [1]

Derailment #4: Bottomless Issues

Sometimes people show up for sessions with a laundry list of issues: "Five work projects are off the rails, I had a confrontation with a colleague, my daughter won't speak to me, and I can't seem to get an exercise routine going!"

When you lay it all on your coach at the beginning of the session, your coach may launch into helper mode. Since they need to start somewhere and you presented all your challenges as equal, the tendency is to latch onto the easiest issue and tackle it first: "You can't seem to get an exercise routine going, you say? What have you tried thus far?"

Having this conversation may or may not be valuable to you. If you already spent four hours researching local fitness studios, found a personal trainer you like, and finally carved out time for three workouts a week, it wouldn't make sense to devote precious coaching time to discussing all of these things. Of course, exercise may still be a real challenge at this point in your life, but talking about it in the session may not be the best use of your time.

---

1 https://thework.com/instruction-the-work-byron-katie/

Some clients show up to sessions with a proliferation of challenges because they are easily distracted; they have a lot of thoughts swimming around in their head, competing for attention. Others have a misunderstanding that in order to get the most value possible out of every single session, they must show up with a litany of issues. And sometimes people are just overwhelmed by everything that's going on in their life and they haven't taken a chance to sit down and think through priorities. This can cause a coach to latch onto something that they find compelling or know how to help with, which may not be the most important thing to focus on to move progress forward. No matter the cause, it can be hard for coaches to weed through all of a client's problems and pinpoint the one that's most important at that particular moment.

Tips for Avoiding This Derailment:

Before each session, ask yourself, "If I could only work on one thing, what would it be?" Decide on your answer before your meeting and let your coach know at the top of the session. And if your coach begins to ask you questions about something that isn't a top priority for you, by all means, speak up (e.g., "That sounds like a great topic and working on that issue is important to me, but there are other things that I'm having a harder time with, and I'd like to focus on those instead.").

Derailment #5: Entering the Friend Zone

In most situations, as you get to know someone, you develop an increasingly casual, social style. As you learn more about each other's lives, it almost feels awkward not to ask how their kid did on that big science project or whether they're planning any big trips for the holiday weekend. Even in business relationships, it can be considered rude to get right down to business instead of engaging in at least a minute or two of perfunctory chitchat. All that's fine, but it eats into your valuable coaching time.

It's important to have emotional boundaries within coaching relationships. As you confide in your coach and share your deepest thoughts and desires, the way you feel about that person can shift. It may start to feel more like a friendship or mentorship than a relationship where you are paying for one-on-one time to improve your life. It's great to develop rapport with your coach and feel safe and comfortable, but keep in mind that falling into the friendship zone may hinder your ability to get the most out of your coaching sessions.

Tips for Avoiding This Derailment

Work on developing other positive relationships with people you can confide in. When you can talk about things going on in your life with friends or family members, you are less likely to lean on your coach for filling that gap.

Also, be professional from the very beginning, and do your best to maintain that throughout your sessions. If you feel the tone of your sessions begin to shift, as with other derailments, speak up. It is in your best interest to maintain a level of decorum that befits your coaching relationship in order for you both to stay focused. Coaches can fall victim to this as well, so bringing it up and explaining your intentions is a great way to help keep your sessions on track.

Derailment #6: Telling Unnecessary Stories

Sometimes people dominate their coaching sessions by sharing stories about things that happened to them. Maybe they're eager to talk about it with someone who will give them undivided attention and the details are just too good not to share. That's all well and fine—unless telling the story isn't necessary for getting help with their goals.

Talking and venting can feel good in the moment, but you're probably paying a decent chunk of money for coaching and have important objectives you want to achieve. It's a slippery slope if you head down the path of wasting time on unnecessary storytelling. It can also put your coach in a tricky spot because they are being respectful and listening to you, but they don't know how relevant the story will truly be for the coaching conversation.

Tips for Avoiding This Derailment

Do you consider yourself to be a "talker"? If so, you need to become hyperaware of how you're sharing with your coach. Focus on the main point of the conversation and what the coach needs to know in order to facilitate the conversation.

Prepare for your sessions by thinking through what has happened recently and pull out the key facts so you can share a summed-up, CliffsNotes version. This will enable you to get to the heart of the matter quicker. Ask yourself, "Given everything that's happened, what do I want to create?"

Derailment #7: Being on the Edge of Your Own Story

As social creatures, we have been conditioned to adhere to certain norms when it comes to having conversations. When someone asks how we're doing, instead of digging in and discussing the nitty-gritty of a specific challenge, we tend to gloss over details and give a broad view of a range of topics. This is especially true in new relationships, or in conversations with people who aren't part of our inner circle. It might sound something like this: "Charlie's grades are getting better, which is great! He got an A on his last math test. And business this quarter has really picked up, so my whole team has been super busy. We're still working hard to meet our goal for this year, but things are good." In a social setting, you've probably had this kind of conversation a million times. It's typical small talk or chitchat, and it's interesting enough for the other people to stay engaged and ask questions that merely scratch the surface of a variety of topics.

The problem with this kind of conversation in a coaching setting is that it doesn't push the real issues to the forefront. Instead of putting yourself at the center of what you're talking about, you're often on the edge of your very own story. It might feel like you're talking about yourself, but you're really talking about your family, your colleagues, and your company. This is how we have been conditioned to show up in social settings so that we don't seem self-absorbed or bore people with details they don't care about.

Tips for Avoiding This Derailment

Remind yourself that coaching is not a social engagement. You are not there to impress anyone or give off a good impression. You are paying someone to help you improve your life. Before you start talking, ask yourself, "How does this information relate to me and my challenges?"

Derailment #8: Being Distracted During Your Session

You would be amazed at the number of people who think they can have a great coaching session while doing the dishes, driving, checking/sending emails, texting, eating, or boarding an airplane. Just because you can physically talk to another human being while doing something else doesn't mean that it's a good idea! This is especially true when you're having conversations that require actual thought and reflection. If you're prone to multitasking, giving your coach your undivided attention can be a difficult thing, but it will make an enormous difference in getting the most out of your sessions.

Another aspect of distraction in coaching that people don't always recognize is being stuck in the wrong mental state. You can't just flip a switch and immediately turn your brain on for coaching; there's no button to magically open your heart like a flower, instantly exposing your vulnerable core to your coach. Don't treat coaching like just another item on your checklist of tasks to do for the day. If you truly want to go deep during your sessions and effect meaningful change, you need to give the time that you spend with your coach the reverence it deserves.

Tips for Avoiding This Derailment

Allow yourself enough time to get into a relaxed state of mind. We call this practice "grounding," and we highly recommend doing it right before your sessions or at the very beginning of your sessions with your coach. Experiment and find what works best for you. It can be as simple as deep breathing, stretching, or a short meditation. Any type of transitional ritual that signals the beginning of your session will help clear your head in order to better focus on the present moment.

For virtual coaching sessions, find a quiet, comfortable spot where other people can't hear what you're saying. Close out of your inbox and silence notifications on your phone, watch, and computer. Have you eliminated all distractions in your environment? On a scale of 1–10, 1 being "You have every browser tab open" and 10 being "You are in a Zen garden," where are you? What level of attention are you committed to during your coaching session? For in-person sessions, arrive early and put your phone and watch on airplane mode.

Schedule your sessions strategically. If Thursdays are already crazy, don't book your only free time with your very precious coaching session. And make sure you eat before your sessions so you aren't tempted to munch on food during your session. Your brain needs fuel, calories, in order to function, just like any other part of your body, and your daily schedule should accommodate for this.

Lastly, if you are feeling sick on the day of your session, call your coach to let them know you are not 100 percent. You need your head in the game and your wits about you in order to get the most out of your coaching.

A Few Final Thoughts

After decades of coaching hundreds of people, we've seen all of these derailments play out in a variety of situations. Sometimes it's easy to recognize, and other times it's not that obvious. A client might have a highly productive session one week and then seem like a shadow of their former self the next. We always ask questions to get to the heart of what's going on, but we can only find out as much as clients are willing to share.

Which of these derailers seem like potential issues for you? Spend some time reflecting on how you tend to show up. Are you just going through the motions, like Andy did in his guitar lessons? Our goal is to help you identify the behaviors that could compromise your coaching results. How can you help yourself avoid these derailers or warn your coach to watch out for them?

Though certainly not as dire or dramatic as a real-life train toppling over, if you're mindful about avoiding these potential pitfalls, you can help keep your coaching sessions right on track—which can get you to where you want to be quite a bit faster.

Can you make
coaching the top priority
in your life?

CHAPTER 6

SETTING GROUND RULES

Now that you've made it to this page, let's discuss how to ensure that you and your coach can stay on the same page, which means establishing some basic ground rules that you both adamantly promise to adhere to.

Expectations are the root of all evil. Okay, maybe that's a little melodramatic, but it's not entirely false!

Think about a time when you were disappointed recently. Maybe it took your colleague two weeks to get back to you about an assignment. Or your partner left dirty dishes in the sink... again. Or maybe you had an issue with a software program and needed to get assistance, but customer service was totally unhelpful. You may not be aware of this, but the vast majority of disappointments you have ever faced in your life were rooted in the same thing: *expectations*. You anticipated something different—and in your opinion, better—than what you got.

When you have expectations of another person, it's one-sided; they haven't agreed to do what you want, and it's highly probable that they aren't even aware of how you feel. This can easily create a toxic situation.

Let's take the example of your partner leaving dirty dishes in the sink. Maybe they do it all the time and have no idea that it bothers you because they don't care one way or the other what you do with your dishes. Maybe their philosophy on washing plates and silverware is fundamentally different from yours: wait until the whole sink is full, then load the dishwasher all at once. Neither of you is right or wrong; it's your expectation that's the problem.

If you fail to discuss your preferred method for washing dishes—or that it matters to you in general—it can easily turn into a conflict. You walk around frustrated and resentful. Over time, it turns bitter. You start to judge their character. They're lazy, thoughtless, and selfish. They appreciate nothing you do for them, and maybe you two aren't actually meant to be.

Do you see how quickly that escalated? Now think about how much worse it could be if the expectations were around something more serious than dishes!

Instead of expectations, use co-created agreements. The key difference is that with agreements, both people are aware of what the other one wants, and they have the opportunity to commit or renegotiate.

In coaching, we've found that agreements set the foundation for successful relationships. So much of coaching is based on quality communication, and creating agreements is the perfect place to start down that road together. Collaboration is key here, since you don't want to just tell someone else what you expect them to do. People are much more motivated to follow through with agreements when they have an active role in creating them.

Agreements depersonalize any potential upcoming challenges. If something occurs inside the coaching relationship that either party isn't happy with, it isn't about criticizing the person, it's about going back to the agreements. Instead of stewing, complaining to your friends, or feeling like your opinions went unheard, it's easy to cite the agreements. Then, if you later find you overlooked an important topic that should have had an agreement, it doesn't feel awkward to bring it up because you've already had the initial conversation.

By implementing agreements in our coaching practices, we've seen it make a world of difference for our clients. One reason for this is that it helps people shift away from being at the mercy, or affect, of everyone else. Agreements are empowering because they call for people to take responsibility for their own energy level and success, rather than blaming others. This mentality is powerful. When it comes down to it, you're the only one you can work on. You can't change other people.

In this chapter, we highlight several topics you can discuss with your coach to then form agreements around. There could be many more agreements that would be helpful for your unique coaching relationship, but this is the beginning of a solid list to get you started.

When establishing agreements with your coach, be as creative as possible and think about what will make this the most incredible relationship possible.

How Hot Is Your Burner?

If you've ever played or watched team sports, you've probably seen a wide variety of intensity levels in coaching. Some coaches scream until they're beet-red in the face and fans are legitimately worried they might have a heart attack right there on the sidelines! Other coaches are famous for remaining calm, cool, and collected, rarely raising their voice—even when everything is on the line.

Most players have a predisposition to respond better to one method over the other. That's a key reason certain player-coach combinations are virtually unstoppable, whereas others just don't develop the cohesion needed to be effective.

As you enter into a new coaching relationship, you may want to think about the level of intensity that works best for you. Karen's former coach, Rich Litvin, describes it as "high flame" (high intensity) or "low flame" (low intensity). A great coach meets clients where they are, although they may have a natural style or inclination toward a certain end of the spectrum. It's important to speak up about what you want because it makes a difference in whether you leave your sessions feeling inspired, underwhelmed, or like you just got yelled at by the principal.

Confidentiality

To truly open up in your sessions, let your guard down, and progress toward your goals, you'll need to share information with your coach that you wouldn't feel comfortable telling the whole wide world. How does your coach handle confidentiality? It's wise to ask to ensure that you're both lockstep in agreement. Assuming you've chosen a reputable coach, you shouldn't have to worry about your trust being violated.

That said, coaches do not have the same legal privileges as attorneys, therapists, or doctors when it comes to privacy issues. Throughout our coaching careers, we've heard a number of stories from clients about times they'd engaged in questionable behavior that could have gotten them in trouble with the law. We have strong agreements in place, and clients know that what they tell us does not leave the room. But if coaches are subpoenaed during an investigation, they are required to hand over all their files from sessions.

Since the thought of even going down that road gives us a terrible feeling in the pit of our stomachs, we both made the decision years ago not to take notes on anything remotely questionable, and even more importantly, not to record sessions. We give clients the option to record sessions on their own if they choose, but we don't ever have possession of the files.

If you would benefit from similar agreements with your coach (or a different one), set up those ground rules from the very beginning.

Time-Commitment Boundaries

You know your coach will be available to you during your scheduled sessions, but what about outside of those timeframes? Instead of making assumptions, it's best to understand specifics. For example, if you get into an argument with your boss and want to get advice before the next scheduled session, is it okay to call or text your coach? Would they see this as a bother, where you're overstepping the nature of the relationship, or would they expect you to come to them when pressing issues arise?

Some coaches are available 24/7, almost like an on-call doctor. Others may prefer not to be contacted outside of scheduled sessions unless there is a true emergency. Neither way of working is right or wrong, and most coaches operate somewhere in the middle of those two extremes. It's essential to understand boundaries before entering into a relationship, because a misalignment in expectations can be hard for either party to deal with.

We recommend setting specific guidelines for the following:

- The kinds of situations in which you should contact your coach between sessions
- The method you should use (texts, emails, calls, etc.)
- Time boundaries on reaching out (e.g., no texts after business hours)
- Whether there is a specific format or template for communicating
- How quickly the coach will reply
- Whether additional support is included in the base coaching fee or is an additional charge

Example Policies

Karen:

You have virtually unlimited access to me. What that means is: I'm available to you during my business hours of 9–5:00 MT, Monday–Friday for spot coaching (10 minutes) or quick responses to emails or phone calls. If something bigger is going on and you need more than 10 minutes, we'll discuss a time that may work better for both of us.

I agree to return emails, phone calls, and text messages to you within two days, during business hours. If for some reason I have not responded to you and you need a response right away, please resend your email, text, or call me on my cell phone.

Alex:

My preference is to use emails only when communicating with you. I request that you limit the types of emails you send to me while we are working together to the following:

- Time-sensitive communications about an upcoming session (you're running late, etc.), making sure they are labeled "Time Sensitive" in the subject line
- Anything technical in nature (clarification around Zoom, online retreat login, scheduling, etc.)
- Updates on assignments or actions we agreed you would send to me
- Any good news, progress, or insights that require no reply from me

When sending an email, please keep it simple and about one topic only. If you're sending me an email that is simply a report, do not combine it with an email that requires my immediate attention.

Please do not request any guidance through email. I do not have the resources to offer written responses in between sessions. If you would like to receive additional coaching about a time-sensitive issue, please let me know. Suggest some dates and times, and I'll see what's possible.

I will reply to your emails within one day, during business hours—even if it is to acknowledge receipt of your email. I request that you do the same with my emails.

Guidelines on Rescheduling

In a perfect world, no one would ever get sick, have car trouble, or accidentally double-book themselves. But since we're operating in the real world, it's important to anticipate scheduling issues and agree on how they should be handled.

When it comes to canceling or moving coaching sessions, your coach is concerned with a few things. Obviously, there could be logistical challenges to finding a new time that works for both parties. There's also the annoyance that comes from being canceled on at the last minute, especially if work has gone into preparing for a session. But the bigger issue—for both you and your coach—is whether you are prioritizing your coaching sessions and taking them seriously.

To get the best results from coaching, it has to be a top priority in your life. In other words, it needs to be more important than almost everything else. We realize that's a bold statement, but hear us out.

Chances are, your coaching sessions won't be every day. And they probably won't be every other day, or maybe not even every week. And it's just as likely that they have a set duration, such as a six-month commitment, or a three-day retreat. When you really look at the number of hours you spend in coaching sessions compared with the rest of your life, it's probably only a tiny fraction of your time. For example, one hour per week is 0.56 percent of your time, and a three-day retreat is 0.82 percent of your time for the year. Considering the amount of value you can derive from dedicating less than 1 percent of your life to something, it's wise to prioritize it. Yes, other important things will come up and vie for your attention, such as family visiting from out of town or a big deadline coming up at work. It might seem like a good idea to reschedule your coaching sessions when these kinds of conflicts arise, but it is rarely in your best interest.

With this in mind, obviously there are situations that absolutely warrant a conversation with your coach about rescheduling. For example, if you come down with the flu, it's pretty unlikely that you will feel well enough to have a productive session. If you can't show up and be 100 percent on your game—for whatever reason—you should let your coach know so you can at least discuss it.

From our experience, people can become so committed to coaching—and so afraid of losing their money from forgoing a session—that they don't reschedule even when they should. Karen has had people show up in person at her studio when they were clearly very sick, even though their agreement made it clear that it's preferred to reschedule at the last minute due to illness.

Long story short, make sure you understand your coach's preferences for rescheduling, take your sessions seriously, and don't compromise your health or well-being in the process.

As you move forward in creating powerful agreements with your coach, we definitely recommend having a live and spoken discussion rather than relying on written documents. There's a simple reason for this: It works better. When we talk through things such as punctuality, rescheduling, and preferred intensity level in coaching, it leads to a mutual understanding. We're both present, there's a two-way dialog, and we can get feedback in real time on what matters to the other person. This simply cannot be achieved by skimming written agreements, which often read more like legalese than simple human promises. That's why we both dedicate an hour or more to discussing and co-creating agreements with new clients.

Setting ground rules starts with a few questions, and how you arrive at agreements with your coach is ultimately up to the two of you. Here are a number of questions we have personally found useful in the past to help you get the ball rolling.

Questions for Both You and Your Coach:

- Do you agree that having powerful agreements will benefit our coaching time?
- What does it mean for us to be in "integrity"?
- What are the specifics of our confidentiality agreement?
- Do you require mutual confidentiality?
- What type of environment will you be in when we coach and what do you recommend for me?
- Will you agree to be on time and prepared for all our sessions?
- How much notice do you require if I need to reschedule a session?
- What are the valid reasons for needing to reschedule a session?
- What is the underlying spirit of how we will relate to one another?
- What is your commitment regarding how you will show up for coaching sessions?
- Is there any language we both agree should not be used in our sessions (e.g., no effin' f-bombs)?

- What will we do if the coaching isn't working for one of us?
- How will we create a professional relationship and avoid social chatting?
- Technically, how will you be coaching (in-person, via video, phone)?
- Will the recording of our sessions be permitted?
- How do you prefer to be contacted between sessions (phone, text, email, video)?
- What happens if I'm feeling sick?

Questions Just for Your Coach:

- What happens if I want to stop coaching or take a pause?
- Do you provide refunds for extenuating circumstances? If so, what qualifies as one?
- What if something were to happen to you and you could no longer coach me?
- How much time should I allow between sessions for reflection and integration?
- How would you suggest that I best prepare for our sessions?
- Will I need a notebook for tracking our progress?
- May I contact you between sessions? If so, how will that work?
- How can I feel like this is a sacred and safe space for me to share and be fully transparent?

- Do you provide tips, strategy, and advice besides coaching?
- Will there be homework or practices between sessions?
- How do you handle insights that are uncovered between sessions?
- Who is responsible for the results of our coaching?
- How do you manage accountability?
- How will we be scheduling our sessions? In advance? Same day/same time?
- What is your agreement with me in terms of returning emails, phone calls, text messages?
- What do you look for in a client who is coachable (i.e., how can I help us succeed)?
- Will you seek my permission before you share difficult information with me?
- What happens if I show up to a session unprepared?
- Will we be working on a specific plan for the coaching?
- If my company is paying for the coaching, how will you manage confidentiality with my manager?
- How will feedback and learning be managed with my organization?

Again, you and your coach are coauthoring these agreements and ground rules together. So use the questions that resonate for the two of you and feel free to dismiss any others that don't. But whatever you do, don't skip over this very critical first step. Simply put, agreements are the most important aspect of building a successful and long-term relationship with your coach.

The One Big Begging Question for You

Can you make coaching the top priority in your life? It's not just the coaching that you're prioritizing—you are prioritizing positive change and powerful personal transformation. It's not only what you are doing in life, but who you are being throughout the day. Your commitment is to positive changes inside and out, your relationships with loved ones, and your mental, physical, and spiritual well-being. That's precisely what you are accomplishing when you prioritize your coaching. By making your coaching the top priority, you become better and more mindful about prepping for each session and being more courageous and thoughtful about what to bring. You are less inclined to cancel a session when something "more important" comes up because nothing is actually more important than you.

Certainly, setting ground rules isn't something anyone would ever consider "fun." But it will empower the two of you to always treat each other with respect. Plus, it's your ticket to always hitting the ground running.

"Be in consistent,
conscious creation."

—Steve Hardison

CHAPTER 7

TAKING ACTION

Now, it might seem like being in a relationship with a coach is just about sitting around talking. While that is a fundamental part of the process, it couldn't be much further from the truth. The ultimate goal is to translate those insights you will gain with your coach's help into concrete actions. Actions that will help you bring changes and improvements into your life.

As you work with your coach, you'll discuss opportunities, challenges, and everything in between. Sometimes you'll work on the areas you expected, and other times coaching will lead you in directions you hadn't anticipated. The most powerful moments in coaching will feel like a lightbulb suddenly switched on in your brain, illuminating a new realization for the first time.

Years ago, Karen began working with Peter, the VP of a pharmaceutical company. She asked him to tell her about himself so they could get to know each other and begin to clarify his goals. Peter said he was primarily focused on professional development at that point in his life, and that he had been through some challenging times in the past. He had struggled with alcoholism for more than half his life, and when his five-year-old son passed away from a terminal illness a decade earlier, his drinking got even worse. He became accustomed to working 60-hour weeks and drinking at the end of each day, just trying to get past the trauma of what had happened. He was proud to report that he had been sober for three years, but he could still feel his son's death weighing on him every day.

Karen asked how hard the situation was on his wife, who was then a stay-at-home mom, to which Peter replied that he and his wife had never really talked about their son's death. At first, Karen thought she'd misunderstood him.

"So you and your wife don't really talk about it anymore, now that so much time has passed?" she inquired.

"No, we never talked about it at all," he clarified. "Our son passed away, just like his doctors told us he would, and then he was gone. We both grieved in our own way, but we never spoke about it."

Karen and Peter discussed what that must have been like for Peter's wife, and he began crying. He said that he wished he had been more attentive to his wife's emotional needs instead of escaping to the office and leaving her in an empty house all week. After 10 years, this realization was a major breakthrough.

Karen suggested that Peter call his wife right then and there to tell her what he'd just shared. Karen left the room while the couple spoke, and afterward Peter filled her in on what happened. Peter's wife told him that she thought all those years of alcoholism had left him emotionally stunted, and he agreed. Spending so much time inebriated from such a young age, he'd never fully acknowledged his emotions or his subsequent grief, which had also made him emotionally unavailable to his wife or anyone else. There were a lot of tears that afternoon, and the conversations sparked an immediate transformation in Peter's marriage, as well as other areas of his life.

No matter what you talk about with your coach or how good it makes you feel during sessions, it is essential to understand that this is only the first step in a two-part process to drive change.

The reason coaching is so powerful is it can inspire you to take life-changing action. Instead of continuing on your default path, coaching helps you understand how to make the changes that will set you on your chosen path. But for coaching to truly make an impact in your life, you have to actually do something different.

Lightbulb Moment + Action = Transformative Change

What follows are some key strategies for driving meaningful action from your sessions. You have a lot of flexibility in how you implement these best practices, but no matter your goals or situation, action needs to be a top priority.

Co-create Action Items

Make it your objective to leave each coaching session with at least one specific action item you can accomplish before the next session. Whenever possible, co-create these action items with your coach rather than going it alone. By collaborating, you're likely to get ideas you never would have come up with on your own. Another benefit is that your coach's suggestions could challenge you and get you out of your comfort zone, which is where you'll experience swift transformation.

An interesting example of this is when Karen's former coach, Rich Litvin, discovered that Karen was wasting a lot of time and energy caring what people thought about her. Always one to keep things interesting, Rich suggested that Karen dress up like a homeless person, spend a full day out in public, and observe how people reacted to her. Doing so, he said, would help shift her mindset to stop worrying about people judging her. Initially, Karen wasn't pleased with this suggestion, but she agreed to do it anyway. She trusted Rich implicitly, and deep down she knew there was some wisdom in this experiment.

One morning, she put on a ratty bathrobe, smeared dark makeup under her eyes, left her wavy hair wild, and headed to the mall with a few old bags in tow. She spent the first few hours mortified and very self-conscious, but she soon realized how kind people were being to her even though many stared. When she went into stores, the salespeople were polite and helpful. No one yelled at her, made fun of her, or told her to get out. At one point, she sat on a bench next to a man, and he immediately got up and moved away. Karen smiled and thought to herself, "Even though he judged me, I'm still safe."

Ever since this unique day, Karen has drawn upon the experience whenever she's started to feel like maybe she's being judged or caring too much about what other people think. She realizes that other people's opinions won't hurt her, and that no matter what people think, she's safe. The experience was transformative—to say the least! And it's safe to say she never would have thought of it or done it on her own.

When it comes to co-creating action steps, many coaches bake it into their sessions. But if your coach doesn't always prompt you to identify specific steps to take as a result of what you learned in a session, it's smart to proactively drive this conversation. Say you want to make sure you have something to work on between sessions, and that you would love insight on what would make the biggest difference. Ideally, you want the actions to be based on an insight, discovery, or lightbulb moment you had during the session. Spending the last 10–15 minutes of each session talking about action steps is certainly a best practice.

Stay Organized

Taking action after your coaching sessions sounds simple in theory, but putting it into practice can be surprisingly complex. To start, you have to remember your moments of insight and the actions you planned on taking based on what you learned. This may seem crystal-clear during a session, but a couple of days later, things can get a little fuzzy. Let your coach know if this is an area where you struggle. Having that insight will help your coach better serve you.

When you can't quite put your finger on exactly what you need to do, coaching is unlikely to drive real change in your life. That's why staying organized is vital to your success. There are a myriad of ways to record and track your ideas and progress. Here are a few tools and strategies to get you started.

Tools for Staying Organized

Play Back the Highlight Reel

Give yourself the time and space to replay your coaching session in your mind's eye, just like top athletes do after a big game. Give your coaching session a three-to-five-word theme, such as, "I Create My World" so that you'll be able to recall it from memory. Jot down your insights and note what actions you are committing to taking because of the session.

Recordings

If your coach allows you to record your sessions, you might find it valuable to watch or listen to them later and take notes. Doing so would also ensure that you can go back and reference a certain point in the discussion if you have trouble remembering what you or your coach said. You could also jot down a specific time during the session to make it easier to go back and reference.

Journal or Notes Document

We recommend having a dedicated space to keep your coaching notes so they are always in one place. Karen usually gifts new clients an elegant notebook they can use throughout their relationship, since it can be so helpful for staying organized. If you prefer electronic notes, you can use an app on your phone or a running Word or Google doc. Between sessions, use this dedicated space to keep track of anything you need to bring up to your coach. It will help you both prioritize your most pressing challenges and use your session time more effectively.

Spreadsheet

Sometimes it's helpful to use the rows in a spreadsheet to list your action steps and the columns for phases of completion, which can make it easier to track multiple priorities that are in various stages.

Mind Map

Some people find mind mapping to be effective when it comes to generating ideas. Try it for brainstorming various challenges and deciding what to discuss with your coach.

Calendar Invitations

Good old-fashioned time blocking can be exactly what you need to ensure you set aside the time needed to complete your action items.

Learning Styles

People primarily learn in one of three ways: by seeing, hearing, or doing. It's incredibly important to know how you learn best so that you can put your learning style into practice for your action items. For example, if you learn by hearing, you may not need to take many notes during your sessions. Instead, listening to your recordings could help cement ideas in your brain. On the flip side, if you learn by doing, you might have trouble committing things to memory unless you go through the act of writing them down.

Not all actions have to be physical. Sometimes just thinking differently is enough to spark change. For example, you may discover in a session that you aren't a particularly good listener. You tend to tune out when people are talking, and because of that, your relationships suffer. Your action steps after this realization might be to become more attentive during conversations, stay focused, and later reflect on what was said so that you can better retain the information. These actions are thought-based practices, but they're just as powerful as physical actions.

Here are a few other examples of thought-based practices that can drive powerful change:

- Focusing on positive over negative
- Giving others the benefit of the doubt
- Practicing gratitude
- Listening without judgment
- Being intentional about positive self-talk
- Completing this sentence: "I forgive myself for judging myself as _____, for the truth is _____."

When working with your coach, keep in mind that actions related to mindset shifts can be difficult to track. How will you know if you've successfully focused on the positive over the negative? Did you really listen without judgment? Pick an area of your life in which these mindset shifts could be a benefit (or ones in which those frames of mind are lacking). Use these areas to practice so you can set tangible and measurable goals within them.

Alex once had a client who struggled with rushing, and in order to not feel harried or stressed, tended to focus excessively on getting everything done quickly. She felt overwhelmed constantly shifting from first gear to fifth with everything in her life all at once. Alex had her pick an easy, no-risk area of her life to practice on and begin spending half an hour washing the dishes, instead of the 15 minutes she normally took. She paid attention to each dish and even set a timer to go off during the half hour in order to catch herself whenever she was clenching her gut or found herself racing to finish. She also focused on trying to stop leaning forward—a physical manifestation of her rushing that was hurting her spine—by placing a book on top of her head to ensure she had good posture at the sink. In this case, a vague mindset shift such as "no rushing" was made tangible and measurable, with noticeable, trackable differences. As can be expected, such a concentrated training focus started to influence her pace both in other areas of her life and at work. That doesn't mean everything was easy-peasy for her from then on, but it was a good start.

Timing Is Everything

Right after meeting with your coach, you will have plenty of new ideas fresh in your mind, and there's a good chance you will feel inspired. This is the perfect time to review your notes or to-do list and start making progress. Block off 30–60 minutes right after your sessions to work independently on your coaching actions. Steve Chandler calls this time period the "integration hour." If you decided in your coaching session that you need to initiate a crucial conversation with your boss, you can use your integration time to send an email and request a meeting. Or if your biggest takeaway is the need to carve out more quality time with your kids, use your integration to make dinner reservations at a place they love, or talk with your assistant about blocking off more personal time on your calendar.

Doing this kind of work immediately after a session is ideal because it gives you momentum. When you get things done quicker, you experience the benefits sooner. You can go into your next coaching session feeling even more inspired because you already nailed the tough conversation with your boss or enjoyed a much-needed night out with your kids. And after your next session, you may be ready to move forward with new action items instead of continuing to work on the same things.

Clients who effectively leverage their integration time are able to accomplish many goals in a small amount of time. One of Karen's most productive clients drove an hour each way to meet at her studio. He used the commute time before his sessions to reflect on the previous week and how he took action, and to consider what he wanted to focus on that day. After each session, he would think back through his conversation with Karen and the actions he planned to take for the upcoming week. This proved to be an incredibly effective way to prepare for sessions and make the most of his time, as well as commit action plans to memory.

The transformative power of coaching may feel like it's happening during your one-on-one sessions when you have a sudden realization, breakthrough, or a brand-new perspective that changes how you view yourself and the world around you. We don't want to downplay the significance of those eureka experiences, but the real miracles happen when you take what you learn in coaching sessions and apply it to your life. In other words, you do something differently as a result of coaching. This is how you steer off of your default path and onto your created path.

Taking Action

As you think more about getting the most out of coaching, focus on what happens between your sessions. When Alex studied at a monastery, they often said, "There can be no change in consciousness without a change in behavior." If you can keep your action steps top of mind and continue putting in effort on your own, you'll see a bigger payoff faster.

Are you ready to take action now? Turn to the next chapter.

"The more important a call or action is to our soul's evolution, the more Resistance we will feel toward pursuing it. Resistance has no strength of its own. Every ounce of juice it possesses comes from us. We feed it with power by our fear of it. Master that fear and we conquer Resistance."

—*The War of Art* by
Steven Pressfield

CHAPTER 8

UNDERSTANDING YOUR COMMITMENT

When it comes to coaching, the math is pretty simple. The more you put into it, the more you get out of it. It's all inextricably tied to your overall level of commitment.

If you put some amount of effort into coaching, you will get some results. You'll probably learn a few things about yourself, come up with better ways to approach certain problems, and make progress quicker than you would have on your own. But if you want to get the most out of your coaching, you'll want to slow down, get organized, and begin to implement the best practices described in this book.

Your sessions are only one part of your total commitment. Sessions are what you're paying for, but if your work stops as soon as your coach's door closes behind you, you won't end up "getting what you paid for." If you want meaningful results, you must take what you learned in your sessions, retain the information, and apply it in your life. The reality is that this takes additional time and effort. How much time and effort, you ask? That depends on what you've set out to accomplish.

A friend of ours recently embarked on her first experience working with a coach. She wasn't sure what would be expected of her during the process, so she set aside time for her weekly sessions, but didn't plan on needing much additional time for other work. After only a few short weeks, she found herself feeling a little behind.

She was getting great insights while working with her coach during their sessions, but she was taking only minimal notes. Each week, she meant to watch the recordings of their video calls to get a refresher on what to work on, but she never scheduled it and thus never got around to it. Pretty soon, a lot of her coach's suggestions began fading from her memory, and the prospect of going back through hours and hours of video seemed too daunting.

Our friend said she got better at taking notes during sessions so she could keep track of new ideas, but she was still having trouble fully executing on her action items each week. She knew she could get better results from coaching if she spent her time differently, but it took her a while to get organized and shift other priorities in order to focus on coaching. In thinking about how long it took her to get up to speed, she was disappointed that she hadn't changed things sooner in order to make more progress and maximize the short amount of time she'd had with her coach. (And of course, she didn't share any of this with her coach because she didn't want him to be disappointed with her progress.)

Our friend's problems all stemmed from one thing: not having a good understanding of what to expect. She didn't know what would be needed from a time standpoint, or how to best stay organized. When she fell behind, she got overwhelmed and didn't know how to handle it. It's easy for this happen, and it's why we decided to write this book. We want people to understand the coaching process and what to do when they are ready to fully commit to it.

One of the biggest issues for those new to coaching is figuring out how to wedge it into their already insanely busy schedules. Whatever your situation, you can make room for coaching in your life. Some of the world's busiest leaders work with coaches on an ongoing basis, despite their professional and personal commitments pulling them every which way, every day. That's because coaching takes time. But here's the genuine beauty of it: It also actually gives you time back. Obviously, it can't create more hours in your day, but it can help you become more focused and efficient, and allow you to work on what matters most in reaching your objectives. This is important to understand early on.

Depending on your current responsibilities, you may need to cut back on other commitments so you have enough time and energy to focus on coaching. If you feel like you're already spread thin, this might be a good area to work on almost immediately with your coach. By collaborating on this challenge, your coach can suggest options for you to create a more manageable schedule in order to avoid over-extension. This is what our friend could have done with her coach—had she been honest with him about how she was struggling to keep up with her practices and actions from sessions.

The good news is that you probably won't need multiple hours each week to focus on coaching. If you have that kind of time and want to use it, you can certainly partner with your coach to discuss the actions you could take to get you to your goals faster. However, if you have a limited amount of time between sessions, the best thing you can do is to dedicate that time to coaching. Just think of it as *quality time* as opposed to *quantity time*.

Buffer Time

Your sessions are obviously a top priority in your schedule, but the next-most valuable time on your calendar is the 30 minutes directly before and after your sessions. As we discussed earlier, these time-frames are important for mentally preparing for your sessions and getting started on action items while they are fresh in your mind. When you block off time before and after your sessions, you're creating space for your coaching to fit into your life—not just from a time standpoint, but from a mental and emotional one. You don't want to go into your sessions like you just stumbled off a bus. If you book meetings back-to-back like many people do, you're setting yourself up for that to happen. Instead, just a 30-minute buffer time on each end of your sessions will allow you to show up calm and prepared. Then, you can carry that feeling with you after your sessions as you get organized for what to do next.

While having a minimum of 30 minutes is recommended, you might benefit from carving out even more uninterrupted reflection time around your sessions. For Karen's two-day Accelerators, her clients fly in early and even disconnect from their phones, with the only exception being emergency calls. Clients spend much of their time outside sessions alone and in reflection. This isn't a vacation; it's allowing space to prioritize their lives. Since most people rarely disconnect from their hectic day-to-day responsibilities, the experience of unplugging can be transformative all on its own.

In addition to your session and buffer times, you'll also need to set aside time to complete your agreed-upon actions. Each week, your goal will be to leave your session with at least one action item for something you can do before you meet with your coach again. Don't wait until the end of the day, when you're exhausted and want nothing more than to go to bed, to implement your action steps. Not only will that create subpar outcomes, but it can make coaching start to feel like a burden. Utilize those times of day when you're at your best.

If instead of helping you reach your goals—which is the reason you sought coaching in the first place—it begins to seem like a chore, you need to adjust your mentality. Schedule time to fulfill the commitment that will improve your life. You'll thank yourself later.

That Voice in Your Head

Your coach will challenge you and invite you outside of your comfort zone. This is how you learn and grow. Unfortunately, it's not always the most comfortable place to be, and chances are you'll experience some inner resistance. You might hear a little nagging voice inside your head telling you to just forget about coaching; that it's too hard and time-consuming. In fact, you might have noticed this voice before, when you've gone after a stretch goal, tried something new, or decided to totally put yourself out there. Part of you is excited for change, but that voice is filling you with fear.

When your coach challenges you, that voice will also question your level of commitment. It might tell you that you don't really want to change that bad, and you might even be better off without making the effort. It's up to you to get past this resistance. The busier you are and the more you need help, the worse it can be. When you find yourself in survival mode trying to keep up but your train is already going off the rails, it's natural for the ego to kick in and tell you that trying to solve your problems or create your dreams (through coaching) is your real problem.

When this happens, lean in to coaching even more. If you're feeling overwhelmed, deflated, or even a little lost, your coach can help you get back on track. That's the beauty of coaching: You don't have to travel your path all alone. Tell your coach about that little voice in your head so you can talk about it together. If you need to schedule more time or reserve more energy to be effective, loop in your coach so they can help.

When it comes to making a commitment to coaching, we can boil it down pretty easily. Think about all the positive outcomes that you could experience from coaching: increasing your income, building stronger relationships, maintaining a greater sense of inner peace, etc. What are you willing to forgo in order to capture those actual outcomes? When you properly prioritize, you'll find yourself with plenty of time and energy to commit to coaching.

Not to give up the secret sauce, but unflinching commitment is one of the keys to coaching, no matter what side of the equation you're on.

"Communication solves all problems."

—Steve Chandler

CHAPTER 9

COURSE CORRECTING

S ome embrace the notion that the only one who truly likes change is a wet baby. Yet, change happens all the time, and it's going to occur throughout your coaching as well. While one path may bring you big dividends for a while, other circumstances may intervene. In which case, you need to be prepared for course corrections along the way.

One-on-one coaching can immediately set transformations in motion across many areas of your life. People are often totally blown away by the progress they make in such a short amount of time. Not only do they have a fresh perspective, but they also have tangible outcomes, such as revenue growth in their business, a compensation increase, or a promotion.

But it's important to do a reality check here. Coaching isn't always a mind-blowing, life-changing experience. Sometimes people don't go through a radical transformation in any areas of their life and the process can be a bit of a letdown. Maybe they enjoy their sessions, but after they leave, nothing really changes. Or they don't feel like they are clicking with their coach, and as a result, conversations don't get to the heart of what matters most.

There are a myriad of reasons coaching can be an underwhelming experience, but fortunately, there are just as many ways to correct course. If you're going through the coaching process and feel like you haven't gotten the return on investment you wanted, it's important to address it as soon as possible. In this chapter, we focus on what do to when something doesn't feel quite right with your coaching progress.

Take Responsibility

The first step in correcting your course is to ask yourself whether you've really put your full effort into being coached. Ask yourself top executive coach Marshall Goldsmith's question: "How can I be a better client?" To get the best results, coaching has to be a top priority in your life. Even if you've put in a lot of time and want nothing more than to reach your goals, if you haven't been 100 percent committed, you're limiting your progress.

Below, we've included a brief recap of some best practices for coaching. Read through the list and consider whether you have room for improvement in any of these areas. If so, that's great! Use it as a straightforward way to immediately change your coaching trajectory.

- **Ground rules:** Have you been following the agreements you and your coach signed off on at the beginning of your relationship? Go back and review them to make sure you aren't expecting anything different from what was discussed. If you're unclear about anything or you want to renegotiate the ground rules, just let your coach know.

- **Scheduling:** Are you showing up to sessions on time? Are you prioritizing them when things get hectic, or are you quick to reschedule when something else comes up?

- **Sessions:** Are you making the most out of your session time by avoiding the eight most common derailers?

  1. Not being prepared
  2. Avoiding the real issue
  3. Focusing on others

4. Having bottomless issues
5. Entering the friend zone
6. Telling unnecessary stories
7. Being on the edge of your own story
8. Being distracted during your session

- **Integrations:** Are you blocking time before your sessions for meditation, grounding, or doing whatever you need to do to get in the right headspace? After your sessions, are you saving time to reflect on what you learned and reserving the time to take the actions?

- **Organization:** Are you taking notes on your goals, progress, discoveries, and actions from your coaching sessions? Do you come to sessions with a list of your highest-value challenges?

- **Action:** Are you co-creating specific and measurable goals with your coach on what to do between sessions and following through with the necessary actions?

- **Attitude:** Have you been optimistic about change and willing to accept guidance? When your coach suggests ideas that are new to you, are you remaining open to experimenting and testing? Are you catching yourself whenever you start to take things personally?

Communicate

Coaching can help you initiate honest, productive conversations with the people in your life. If you've been wanting to get something off your chest for years, or simply communicate better with loved ones in order to have your needs met, coaching is an excellent avenue for making those changes. But while you're working on communicating better outside of your sessions, don't overlook the importance of doing so inside your sessions.

Course Correcting

Sometimes people come to think of their coaches as experts; the coach is the leader, and the client is the follower. We want to stress how important it is to avoid this kind of thinking. When you think of yourself as a follower, like you might if you were studying under a teacher, guru, or religious leader, it's easy to avoid discussing what's truly on your mind, instead deferring to the leader to guide you and thus solve your problems. If you do this in one-on-one coaching, you will not get the best result. That's because there isn't one "right" answer for your life. It's your journey, so you get to drive. Your coach is there to help navigate you to wherever you want to go, but they can't choose the path for you. They also can't read your mind.

If you find yourself wishing that your coach would do something different, by all means share your thoughts. It gives your coach the opportunity to adjust. The key to making this an easy and productive conversation is by turning your complaints into requests.

A coach Karen worked with as an apprentice, for instance, got some powerful feedback from his client that helped him adjust how he shows up in sessions. The client sent the coach an email saying that he liked working with him much better when he was "soft and slow as opposed to fierce." He asked if it would be possible for the coach to dial his intensity down a bit to make the sessions less threatening. The coach was happy to "lower the flame on the burner," and the two went on to form an even deeper relationship.

This is the perfect example of two people initially having their wires crossed. It happens every so often. Instead of stewing about it, getting offended, or throwing in the towel and looking for a new coach, the client made the smart decision to communicate how he felt. Instead of complaining about what had happened, he made a simple request that the coach do something different, and they moved past the issue immediately with grace and ease.

Moving On from Your Coaching Relationship

As we evolve, change is inevitable. A favorite toy loses its luster, a "spacious" starter home becomes packed to the gills, and a promising new job ultimately feels like it's holding us back. When something no longer serves us, it's time to move on.

It's possible to view relationships through a similar lens, but we advise you to be cautious. It takes time for relationships to build and grow. Sometimes you click with people immediately, but other times it's a slow burn. You might have experienced this in the past with classmates, colleagues, or teachers. In the beginning, you didn't know any of those people from Adam—and you never expected them to leave such a lasting impression on you. But somehow, things changed. You got to know people; they got to know you, and new facets of your relationship began to unfold. Looking back, it may even be hard to see that person as you once did—a stranger—since they have become such a meaningful part of your life.

Coaching is like that too. However, the dynamic is unique because you are paying your coach—often a significant investment—to help you transform your life. The stakes are higher than other relationships in which you haven't chosen from the onset to invest your time and money.

Having so much skin in the game tends to make people evaluate their coach with a critical eye; a plateau in progress or a difference of opinion becomes a red flag that something isn't working. Instead of giving their coach the benefit of the doubt, they wonder if it's time to move on and find someone else.

There's nothing wrong with assessing your relationship with your coach, but becoming impatient isn't going to benefit you. When you have a talented coach, chances are low that you will outgrow them, especially in the short term. There is great value in creating breadth and depth in your relationship with your coach. If you aren't getting the results you want, it's much more likely that something else about the coaching relationship—or your life—needs to change, rather than you swapping out your coach.

Karen, who typically coaches her clients across multiple years, had been working in an apprenticeship program with James, an executive coach, for almost three years when he came to her about potentially ending their coaching relationship. James said he might want to work with a male coach instead.

Karen was curious as to why he felt this way, so they had an honest conversation about it. James explained that ever since he was a kid, he'd felt like he was lacking strong male role models. He thought having a male coach might be a good way to fill that gap. Karen was surprised by this explanation, since she'd experienced her client as a powerful man who was transforming the lives of many other men through his own coaching practice. Nevertheless, Karen stayed curious. She began to slow James down and ask him about the men in his life.

The conversation was a great way to dive into one of James's deepest desires, which was to improve the connection and intimacy of his relationship with his 103-year-old grandfather, who was still in his life. Karen and James focused on this in the next sessions.

Together, they came to the realization that James's grandfather had always been devoted to him, but he was outspoken whenever he thought James made poor decisions. In other words, he called James out when he felt he wasn't living up to his full potential. He did it out of love, but it rubbed James the wrong way. He felt like his grandfather was often criticizing him, so he started avoiding him. Over the years, they grew apart, which is what tends to happen when you routinely dodge calls or act like you are too busy.

James finally understood that he did have a powerful male role model in his life, but he had been pushing him away. Once he made this realization, he was able to intentionally rekindle his relationship with his grandfather. He no longer felt the need for a new male role model, and he found out that he still had more to learn from a female coach. He decided to sign on to work with Karen for another two years.

Had James not been able to talk to Karen honestly about how he felt like he was outgrowing their relationship, things would have gone very differently. He could have stopped working with Karen without giving her an explanation, and then would have either delayed or completely missed out on having the breakthrough about his grandfather. Instead, he would have invested more time and energy into finding a new coach and building that relationship from scratch. Even if the male coach turned into a positive role model, would it have been better than rekindling the relationship with his grandfather?

Before you decide to call it quits with your coach, the best thing you can possibly do is have an open and honest conversation with them about your feelings. If you feel like you've gone as far as you can with them, explore that in a session.

Coaching can sometimes be an imperfect process. If you haven't hit your stride with coaching, partner with your coach to get on the right track. You would be amazed at what two people can accomplish when they are committed to fully showing up and working through challenges.

So before you deliver that "Welcome to Dumpsville, population: you" message, give both of you a chance by having an open, honest, and frank discussion with your coach. It's possible that a simple course correction, either small or large, may be all you need to keep moving forward together toward that progress you deserve.

Coaching empowers you
to go after the life you
want to create.

CHAPTER 10

KEEP CREATING YOUR FUTURE

A chieving the improvements you want in life might seem like a destination, but it really is more of a continuum. Brick by brick, you keep building a stronger foundation so that you continue to reach higher and capture a brighter future. Which is why it's critical that you just keep on creating. The right coach can help you with that.

A key reason coaching can be a great long-term solution is it helps you see your blind spots. When you go after a goal, you can't always see what's keeping you from reaching it. Without an outside perspective, it's easy to continue down the same path, struggle, and eventually give up. But when a coach is working with you to reach your goals, they enable you to see things you might have never noticed on your own.

Karen has hired and worked with a handful of coaches consistently since 2007. That's many years and thousands upon thousands of dollars invested in her personal growth and professional development. Some people might think that having this kind of ongoing support isn't necessary, that people should, at some point, "graduate" from a learning or coaching arrangement. But for Karen, it's come down to excellence and mastery of her profession, and whether she's deriving value from having a coach. On a regular basis, she evaluates the actions she's taken as a result of coaching. If she can attribute positive changes in her life, either tangible or intangible, she knows that investing in coaching has been worth it, and she should continue on the same path.

In truth, she continues to find a tremendous amount of value in all areas of her life from coaching. Not only did Karen's coaches help her as a business entrepreneur and coach, but they also focused their coaching on who she was being in every aspect of her life.

Over the five years Karen worked with Steve Chandler, their coaching relationship only became richer. And when her skills improved, Steve continued to meet her where she was and encouraged her to strive for even more.

Maintaining Momentum

When you think about coaching in the traditional sense—through a sports lens—you see the same thing happening with athletes across the board. When people learn about any new sport, having a coach makes a huge difference. And as they become skilled enough to compete, they don't suddenly fire them—that's when they need them even more! Athletes understand coaching is a key driver of their success, and will continue to be that way as long as they want to keep improving. Just like athletes can attribute their performance to certain skills they learned or honed from working with a coach, so can you.

Maybe you've been trying to grow your business, and it seems like you've tried everything—improving your customer service, hiring better, adjusting your pricing, and so on—but nothing has gotten you to the next level like you hoped. A coach might be able to see that what's holding you back from growth is actually your company's sales presentations. Maybe that's the key step in bringing in new business—which isn't going as well as it should—and you simply overlooked it.

You would be amazed at how often we have breakthroughs such as this with clients—repeatedly over many months or years. We start with one challenge, and after we've conquered it, we move on to the next. Gaining this kind of momentum is actually exciting. Our clients see that they are able to get past long-term issues, and it encourages them to keep leveling up. Small changes start to ripple across all areas of their life, and soon enough, they are in a totally different place than when they started being coached.

When you achieve this kind of breakthrough and your coaching contract is coming to an end, you have two choices: You can either stop or keep going. Sometimes it's a difficult decision. At the moment, you might be thrilled with your progress, and it can seem like your work is done. Maybe coaching was a big investment, both in terms of money and time, and you aren't sure if it's necessary to keep going. Maybe you think you can keep up the momentum on your own. We hear you! We've seen people struggle with the decision of whether to continue coaching, take a break, or check it off their list of completed projects.

First, put your new normal into perspective. It's funny how quickly small improvements can become the new normal, and you forget what things were like before you started working with your coach. That's why we recommend tracking your aha moments and action steps and reviewing them regularly with your coach. This will both help you see how far you've come and accurately assess your return on investment from coaching.

Next, evaluate your goals. Do you still have more you want to achieve? Is there a gap between your current life and the life you want to create? If so, your coaching journey might not be over. Consider the changes you would like to make in your life over the next several months and whether working with a coach would help you create that reality.

Then, ask yourself if your coaching relationship has evolved. Do you have good chemistry with your coach? Do they know the kind of resistance or limiting beliefs you fall for, and see the possibilities in your life that you don't see? If yes, these are positive signs that you work well together. If you are on a good path for making progress, and your coach is your thinking partner and confidant, it's probably worth holding on to that relationship and maintaining your trajectory.

Are you feeling too busy? We often hear our clients say that they are getting too busy for coaching. In our experience, the exact opposite is most often true. The busier you are, the more you need a coach to help you streamline your own effectiveness, resourcefulness, and creativity. If being overextended is a pain point, let your coach know immediately so you can get help working through it.

Do you trust your gut? Your friends, partner, and colleagues will have their own opinions about coaching. They may not understand why your sessions are such a high priority in your life, and might question whether it's worth the investment. The only person who can truly evaluate how well coaching is helping you is *you*. Trust your gut.

You entered into a coaching relationship because you wanted to change your life. Whether your primary focus was your career, relationships, leadership skills, or anything else under the sun, you wanted to shift away from your default path and onto your chosen path. When you optimize your coaching experience, anything is possible.

Stay Open

Because we are so passionate about your success, it's important for us to provide thorough advice on how to get the most out of your coaching. In doing so, we are giving you what seems like a lot to do! If you haven't started working with your coach yet, or the relationship is still in its infancy, you might even be a little intimidated by all the best practices in this book, or the coaching investment in and of itself.

Our best piece of encouragement is stay open. If you can do this, we are confident your hard work and commitment to coaching will pay off! You have the ability to transform anything you have ever dared to dream. And in our experience, the results from coaching are typically beyond what our clients think they could ever achieve.

In writing this book, we set out to teach you how to get the most out of coaching. But we also haven't yet mentioned another major benefit of going on this journey with us: You can apply this process to drive more happiness, growth, and fulfillment across all aspects of your life. The steps described in this book are the same actions that will lead you to success across a range of interests and pursuits throughout your life. Coaching empowers you to go after the life you want to create.

Thank you for joining us on the journey through this book! We hope your own personal journey is even more rewarding.

Acknowledgements

From Karen

The most extraordinary and fulfilling achievements in my life have always been in collaboration with others. I am beyond grateful to all of you.

To my incredible partner, Alex, your relentless love, sense of humor, and kindness are such treasures. I love our early morning walks with Prince Jax during which the concept of this book was born. To my two adult children, Dustin and Alexa, who continue to inspire me each day. To my dad, who always encouraged me to stay curious and believe in myself. To my late mom, for her unrelenting love.

Such heartfelt gratitude to my coach of many years, Steve Chandler. You have been my rock for this book and one of the biggest influences in my life. To Rich Litvin, for coming into my world and modeling for me world-class coaching and how to show up as a client. To my coach, Steve Hardison, your love, kindness, and fierce heart have created the potential for my further development as a coach and client.

I have such a grateful heart for my apprentice coaches who have inspired me to keep stretching and learning during the writing of this book: Yanush Cherkis, Sue Barber, Justin Perkins, Matt Hogan, Garrick Isert, and Gretchen Hydo. All of you helped to inform this book.

Such gratitude to my former clients and colleagues who agreed to be interviewed for this book. All of them stood out to me as experts in getting the most out of coaching and gave their time freely. Thank you, Don Dew, Dr. Laurie Addison, Scott Aller, Steve Riegel, Josh Morin, and Peter Feer.

To my coaching colleagues over the past five years with Steve Chandler in the M6: Tina Quinn, Kamin Samuel Bell, Devon Bandison, Carolyn Freyer-Jones, Mo Goldman, Melissa Black Ford, Sherry Welsh, and Gary Mahler. I learned from each of you how to be not only be a better coach, but a better client!

To Amelia Forczak for your talent and patience in helping two powerful and opinionated personalities bring together in one voice this field guide for our clients.

To you, our dear reader, whether you are a coach or a client of a coach. Our intention is to create a tremendous impact for you in a void we saw in the profession. Thank you for the generosity of your time, attention, and heart. I hope you can take some of the wisdom in this book and apply it to your life immediately. My last wish is for that song from the rock opera *Tommy* to have stopped playing in your head! Thank you, Steve Chandler, for your endless playlist of metaphors!

From Alex

Thank you to my beautiful, loving, brilliant, and compassionate partner, Karen Davis. You are my beacon of light, champion, and true love.

Thank you and "deep Gasshō" to my teacher, the monastery, the monks, the Buddha, the teachings, the teachers, and all sentient beings for the best life training and education I could ever ask for. I will always affectionately refer to my 14 years of training at the Zen monastery as my "profound spiritual bootcamp."

Thank you to Steve Chandler for your guidance, support, friendship, encouragement, and generosity. You have always been a vocal advocate for meditation, and my work in particular. I am so thankful I got to meet and spend time with you at your coaching prosperity school: The ACS.

Thank you to the grads who completed my online retreats: "Heart-to-Heart: Compassionate Self-Mentoring," "Help Yourself to Change," and "Your Practice: The Zen Life Group Coaching Program." You are a light unto the world. We need more of you doing the deep inner work!

And finally—last, but nowhere near least—my biggest thank you goes to my mother and father, Mom and Dad. Talk about selfless service and undying, unconditional love. You may not have always understood some of the choices I made in my life, but you always loved me through them. I love you so much!

From Karen and Alex

Thank you—the client, the coachee, the student—the one who wants to do better, live better, be happier, and rock this one precious life you've been given. May every experience you have along the path enlighten you.

Other Books By Alex Mill

A Shift to Love: Zen Stories and Lessons

Living the Zen Life: Practicing Conscious, Compassionate Awareness (Volumes One–Three)

Meditation and Reinventing Yourself

Practicing Presence: Learning the Art of Directing the Attention!

Other Books Coauthored By Karen Davis

When All Boats Rise: 12 Coaches on Service as the Heart of a Thriving Practice

Unconventional Wisdom: Stories Beyond the Mind to Awaken the Heart

Recommended Reading

Time Warrior: How to Defeat Procrastination, People-Pleasing, Self-Doubt, Over-Commitment, Broken Promises, and Chaos by Steve Chandler

The War of Art by Steven Pressfield

Crazy Good: A Book of Choices by Steve Chandler

100 Ways to Motivate Yourself, Third Edition: Change Your Life Forever by Steve Chandler

The Ultimate Coach by Amy B. Hardison and Alan D. Thompson

The Advice Trap: Be Humble, Stay Curious, and Change the Way You Lead Forever by Michael Bungay Stainer

Being Mortal: Medicine and What Matters in the End by Atul Gawande, Robert Petkoff et al.

Loving What Is: Four Questions That Can Change Your Life by Bryon Katie with Stephen Mitchell et al.

Remembering the Light Within: A Course in Soul Centered Living by Drs. Ron and Mary Hulnick

Daring Greatly: How the Courage to Be Vulnerable Transforms the Way We Live, Love, Parent and Lead by Brené Brown

The Seat of the Soul: 25th Anniversary Edition by Gary Zukav

If you would like to reach Karen, please go to
www.karendaviscoaching.com or
email karen@karendaviscoaching.com

If you would like to reach Alex, please go to his website:
www.zenlife.coach.

Made in the USA
Las Vegas, NV
04 November 2021